PR
MENDIN
IN A BRO

"Of the many wonderful books Patsy has written, this is my new favorite. With her charming candor and a whole sewing basket full of fresh insights, she offers hope to all who need some mending in their lives."

—Robin Jones Gunn,
bestselling author of the Glenbrooke series

"Patsy Clairmont is one of the greatest communicators I know. Whether in speaking or writing, God uses her powerfully to fill thousands of broken hearts with His life and His hope."

—Kathy Troccoli,
singer, speaker, and author of *Different Roads*

"MENDING YOUR HEART IN A BROKEN WORLD is Patsy Clairmont's most outstanding book. She achieves an incomparable balance between brilliant emotional insights and thoroughly entertaining wit."

—Neil Clark Warren,
author of *Make Anger Your Ally*

MENDING YOUR HEART IN A BROKEN WORLD

Finding Comfort in the Scriptures

PATSY CLAIRMONT

WARNER BOOKS

An AOL Time Warner Company

All Scripture quotations, unless otherwise indicated, are taken from the *New* American *Standard Bible*, © copyright 1960, 1968, 1971, 1972, 1973, 1975, 1977. The Lockman Foundation. Used by permission.

Scripture quotations marked NIV are taken from the *Holy Bible, New International Version* ®. NIV ®. Copyright © 1973, 1978, 1984 by International Bible Society. Used by permission of Zondervan Publishing House. All rights reserved.

Scripture quotations marked KJV are taken from the King James Version.

Warner Books, Inc., 1271 Avenue of the Americas, New York, NY 10020

Visit our website at www.twbookmark.com.

 An AOL Time Warner Company

Printed in the United States of America

Originally published in hardcover by Warner Books, Inc.
First Trade Printing: June 2002
10 9 8 7 6 5 4 3 2 1

The Library of Congress has cataloged the hardcover edition as follows:

Clairmont, Patsy.
    Mending your heart in a broken world : finding comfort in the scriptures / Patsy Clairmont.
        p. cm.
    Includes bibliographical references.
    ISBN 0-446-52851-X
    1. Christian life—Anecdotes. 2. Bible. O.T. Nehemiah—Criticism, interpretation, etc. I. Title.

BV4517 .C57 2001
248.8'6—dc21   2001033414

ISBN 0-446- 67923-2 (pbk.)

Book design and text composition by L&G McRee
Cover design by Bernadette Anthony
Front cover photograph by David Sack/FPG

To all who have broken hearts

"Comfort, O comfort My people," says your God.
ISAIAH 40:1

CONTENTS

Mending Your
Heart in a
Broken World

CHAPTER ONE

Tattered Hearts, Topsy-Turvy World

If I had to choose a logo, one that represented my life, it would have to be a U-Haul. The only folks I know who have moved as frequently as my family are the Israelites from the Book of Exodus.

Through almost forty years my husband, Les, and I have hauled our belongings from one dwelling to another at least every five years in search of, uh, manna, I reckon. People ask why we've relocated so often. I've learned to quip, "To keep down the dust bunnies."

The truth is the Exodus bug bit my hubby at a very young age, and he just loves to wander. Oh, we never go far—we've lived in the same town most of our thirty-nine years of marriage. But Les just goes and goes and goes. Like the famous pink rabbit whose batteries keep his furry feet padding around life's landscape, he gives new dimension to the term "bunny hop."

Early in our marriage I didn't mind the hopping around. In fact, it felt like an adventure. But after the first fifteen moves, I grew weary of cardboard boxes and broken stuff.

Honestly, I've never had a move, no matter how close by, that we didn't lose, break, or damage some of our belongings. I've become quite adept at repairing skinned furniture, gluing chipped figurines, and patching fabric tears. Inevitably tables are jammed against doorframes, glass is cracked in transport, and protruding thingamabobs snag cushions.

Once, in a family effort to move our items into a home, we formed a bucket brigade between the truck and the new house to pass along our belongings. In the handoff a world globe was being tossed from one set of youthful hands to another, when it tumbled to the ground, jolted down the driveway, and crashed into the mailbox post. The orb split in two, right along the equator.

"You've broken my world," I whimpered.

The helpers rolled their eyes at my acute case of melodrama.

"Don't worry, honey. I'll glue it back together later," my husband assured me.

Sure enough, after a few days Les, the mobile fix-it man, repaired the cracked globe. Although I must say it never sat properly on its axis again, and I noted, even though great effort had been taken, the hemispheres didn't match up. Also, some noticeable scars were left across the earth's terrain from the raucous journey.

Perhaps your world has been broken in a similar fashion. Perhaps a job loss, a divorce, a serious illness, or a death has split your heart in two.

Ah, herein lies the premise for this book: Can one exist in a fractured world with any sense of a fixed reference? If our hearts and dreams have been broken or scarred by life's journey, how might we recover? Must we be ongoing victims of rocky circumstances, careless people, and deliberate potshots hurled by our enemies? How can we experience comfort in the midst of heartbreak? I know I've asked myself these questions.

Tattered Hearts

Twenty-five years ago, as a young adult, circumstances felt as if they had spun out of control, and I was so emotionally frayed that everyday activities (such as washing dishes) overwhelmed me. Depression, insecurity, fear, guilt, and anger dominated my terrain. And the hemispheres of my brain didn't seem to match up, which left my thoughts scattered and my heart scarred.

My world was reduced to the four walls of my home—actually to the size of my mattress, for I feared to leave the safety of my bed. I waited for God to rescue me. And he did. But not at all in the way I expected. I'll tell you more about that later in the book, but here's a little glimpse at how I still have twinges of aftereffects from that time, when my heart was so damaged.

Last November I spoke at a conference held on a Caribbean cruise ship. Since this was my first cruise, I was a bit apprehensive about leaving land so far behind. I mean, what if we were in surround-sea and I wanted to get off? I don't swim, and I wasn't sure how far one could dog-paddle nor did I want to find out. I'm grateful that, once we set sail (I've always wanted to say that), I loved the sea, and I found even the vigorous waves added a pleasing rhythm to the ride.

At one of our ports, I signed up for a small submarine excursion 125 feet below the water level. When I read about it in the brochure, I thought it would be an adventuresome thing to do, but as we boarded the minuscule, bobbing vehicle, I was having second thoughts. Inside the sub were two long, wooden benches where the passengers sat shoulder-to-shoulder with those next to them and back-to-back with those behind them. Quite cozy. Reminiscent, actually, of sardines tucked ever so friendly-like in an oily can, minus the oil. We all faced windows that allowed us to view the undersea world. As the craft descended, I realized, ready or not, I was committed. Glub, glub, glub.

We witnessed schools of darting fish, strange eels sticking eerily out of the sand like crooked sticks, various sea urchins, and hills and valleys. I was enthralled. I hadn't realized how many dimensions the ocean's terrain offered or how fascinating I would find it to see underwater life skimming by. One of my greatest delights was when a large turtle wafted past us. Those creatures might be bulldozers on land, but in the water they are wondrous sea-angels.

Before I realized it, we were surfacing, and I climbed out, pleased for the experience. But on the way back to the cruise ship, I was surprised to hear comments from some of the other sub participants. "Well, that was disappointing." "I didn't think it was worth the price." "I thought it would be more colorful." "Dull, if you ask me."

I was amazed. Why, I would have paid the price many times over for the watery show. But then I realized that the greatest part of the experience for me was that I had done it at all. Twenty-five years ago, I had collected a myriad of fears and had become an agoraphobic. And even though since then I've traveled a long, open road of freedom, I still have fears to face (like stuffed submarines descending into the ocean). So, while our submarine ride was just a side note for others, for me the excursion was an exhilarating victory. As Louisa May Alcott said, "I am not afraid of storms for I am learning to sail my ship."

Nowadays I travel around the country speaking to thousands of people about the God who sets prisoners free, mends broken hearts, and comforts the hurting, the lonely, and the lost. And I ought to know.

Today I believe in miracles. Out of brokenness can come good: Character can be deepened, relationships can be restored, emotions can be steadied, and a mind can be healed. Now, isn't that miraculous?

Please note: I'm not a counselor or a pastor; I'm merely a cracked pot seeking superglue for my own heart in this topsy-turvy world. As a matter of fact, last year, when upheaval revisited my life, I turned to Scripture in search of healing for my tattered self-image and for counsel regarding some damaged relationships. In the Book of Nehemiah I discovered insight, instruction, and encouragement. In fact, I found it so mentally stabilizing, emotionally comforting, and spiritually enriching that I wanted to share it with others—I wanted to share it with you. I pray that together we can draw from the trying experiences of Nehemiah's people to help us all—even when our world is askew.

Topsy-Turvy World

This broken world is full of hazards and dangers; our daily lives are filled with examples.

"Hold Mommy's hand, and don't let go," a young woman sternly cautioned her wide-eyed child at the grocery store.

"Did you lock the car doors?" a wife quizzed her husband as they entered the neighborhood post office.

"Whatever you do, don't set down your briefcase even for a minute," a coworker reminded her traveling companion at a bustling airport.

"Cover the keypad while you dial," whispered a father to his teenage daughter in a restaurant.

"We'd better stick our packages in the trunk," prompted one shopper to another when they stopped for coffee.

We live in a day when vigilance is necessary even in Small Town, U.S.A., lest we become the next victim in this fractured world. And it only takes one time of being threatened, cheated, or worse, accosted in some harmful way, to cause one's heart to fill with fear and dread. One brick through a windshield, one psycho driver on the freeway, or one desperate gunman, and we are reminded how vulnerable we are.

Recently a woman in her late fifties approached my book table at a conference where I was speaking. She was using a cane, and obviously she had trouble getting around. I noted her struggle, and I figured she had gone through hip surgery. But as we chatted, she told me that she and her husband were dragged from their car, beaten, and left for dead by young men trying to qualify for a gang. She said her husband was still facing several surgeries to fuse his spine. I was stunned at how torn their hearts must be as their world was brutally ripped apart.

Yet it doesn't take strangers, gang members, or thieves to teach us our defenselessness, does it? A reckless parent, a thoughtless teacher, a well-meaning friend, or a beloved child can leave a trail of pain across our tender hearts. Not to mention our own foolish choices, inappropriate responses, and sinful tendencies. Then add life's calamities such as fierce storms, financial reversals, and loved ones' deaths. No, we don't even have to stray out our front doors to find life can be brutal, people can be dangerous, and often we add to the problem.

"Golly, what's the good news?" you ask. "Hurry, please."

Yes, we live in a hazardous world, where jolts and crashes leave us whiplashed and broken. But I believe we will learn from Nehemiah some liberating truths that will enable us to shore up our interior strength, renovate our minds, repair some breaches, and guard our vulnerable hearts. Also, we will enter into victory celebrations, which in contrast to this jagged-edged world, is good news—yes, good news indeed!

Before we begin our journey, let's set the stage for the time period we'll be looking at. Nehemiah lived during the reign of the Persian king Artaxerxes, which was from 464 to 424 B.C. Even though Nehemiah was in the upper echelon of servants because he had access to the Persian king and queen, he was a servant nonetheless. Born into captivity, he had known no other life yet had a deep passion for his Jewish homeland and his people. Jerusalem had lain in ruin for about 150 years, its walls destroyed by enemies, its gates burned, its homes and temple plundered. Its people were too demoralized, fearful, and scattered to attempt to rebuild the city. The broken world of Jerusalem lay heavy on the heart of this servant man, who longed to see the city restored and his people gathered together again. Nehemiah's destiny was established in his name, which means "Jehovah comforts." Jehovah's hand obviously was on

Nehemiah as the servant became not only the leader of his people but also a comforter to them.

The story of how Nehemiah brought God's people together and brought comfort to their war-tattered hearts is found in the Old Testament. Nehemiah's book is situated between the Book of Ezra, who was a priest, and the Book of Esther, who was a queen. A priest, a queen, and a servant . . . yes, God uses individuals from different walks of life to bring solace to his people. And Nehemiah's book, believed to be taken from his personal journals, is written with great warmth. From his emotional response to his people's needs, to his determination to rebuild Jerusalem, we find that Nehemiah, like a well-built wall, was a man of strong convictions and fortitude.

As we enter into Jerusalem's broken world, we'll see how God kindled a passion and a vision in Nehemiah's heart and raised him up not only to rebuild a city and a people but also to touch our troubled hearts.

To help accomplish that purpose, at the close of each chapter, I've written a section called "Heart Menders" that will offer questions designed, first, to help us personally to consider the scriptural truths, drawing them into our minds. Second, the questions are written to stir our hearts toward healing, that we might know God's comfort.

Perhaps you, like me, often are tempted to skitter through material instead of taking the time to pause and reflect on what was said and how it fits inside you. The "Heart Menders" will slow us down for some contemplative moments. If, while you're reading, you feel a twinge of interest in a particular story, quote, question, or Scripture, rest there for a time and ask the Holy Spirit to illuminate your mind. He may want to guide you to a new pinnacle of truth, lift your face to the Father, or enfold you in his tender mercies. And who would want to miss that? Not me! When we are quiet before the Spirit of God, we are far more likely to be aware of his holy nudges, his gentle stirrings, and his tender counsel. I pray that, instead of only gathering information, we would integrate truths into our lives, receiving godly insight, divine healing, and blessed comfort.

NEXT

Nehemiah's world temporarily is turned upside down to reestablish the direction of his life. Hmm, you mean the disastrous can work out to be the miraculous?

CHAPTER TWO

What's in the Cup?

TO DO.

Read Nehemiah 1:1–3.

(*The Book of Nehemiah is located at the back of this book.*)

What enthralls us so about a palace? Is it the wealth, the power, the political sway? Perhaps the idyllic longing to be a prince or a princess and to live happily ever after? I know as a child I sported my share of construction-paper tiaras as I pranced and pirouetted about my kingdom in search of Prince Charming.

Then I grew out of my tiaras and into startling reality. I learned that palaces tend to be dark, drafty, and dank—and so are some of the inhabitants. In fact, we've heard an earful from the media, even of late, regarding royal families' scandalous behavior.

"Tsk, tsk, tsk," we say.

Yet who of us would want our families scrutinized and then have the findings publicized? Holy mote, not me!

Even with my somewhat tainted view of palaces, I confess I'm still drawn to castle gates in hopes of a royal glimpse. In fact, come join me as we peek into a faraway palace and meet one prince of a fellow.

Cushy Job

Our story begins during Bible times in a Persian palace that, for many, was nothing more than a scandalous prison. Often captives were made to serve their enemies, and our hero, Nehemiah, had spent his life serving the Persians.

Still, in the eyes of many, Nehemiah had a cushy job in a plush establishment: He was a royal servant, a cupbearer, in the king's palace. You have to admit it wouldn't be all bad, even if it was a tad drafty, to traipse about palatial halls, to dress in finery, and to dine on the best food in the kingdom.

However, a major downfall did exist in his regal employment, and I do mean downfall. You see, if some radical decided he didn't like the king or wanted to take over the kingdom and managed to slip some poison into His Highness's toddy, it was bye-bye, Nehemiah. If the drink passed the taste test, Nehemiah would present the goblet to the king as an offering. That was the wine server's purpose—to taste the drink and to live or die with the bitter results. Hmm, I guess every job has its drawbacks.

(By the way, when I mentioned Nehemiah's job to my family, I could tell by the look in their eyes that they wished for a cupbearer to taste my kitchen concoctions prior to their ingestion, but alas, they didn't have anyone to go before them as a taster. Much to their amazement, and sometimes mine, they survived.)

Sometimes cupbearers were taken into the king's confidence, which was the case with Nehemiah. We know this because we read in chapter 2 of the Book of Nehemiah that he was not only in the king's presence but also the queen's—a rare honor afforded only the most trusted of staff. This wasn't a guy who just showed up at work and put in the required hours. His trustworthiness served him well as a servant and later would serve him well as a leader of his people.

By reading Nehemiah's account, we see that this esteemed servant was not only reliable, but he also was amiable. In fact, get this: He never showed up at work grouchy or even sad. Whoa, how many of us could say that? (Of course, kings weren't fond of downcast folks and tended to lop off their heads—now there's motivation to stay perky.)

Bad News

But one day Nehemiah received reports about Jerusalem, the city in which his family was captured ever so many years ago. And the news wasn't good. The walls still were down, the burned gates were unreplaced, and the people routed (Neh. 1:3). Jerusalem lay in disrepair, and the people who weren't taken captive by their enemies remained scattered and living in fear. That's when this upbeat bearer of wine and winsomeness hit bottom. Seems the news knocked the smile right off his face.

Nehemiah was more than temporarily stunned by the news; we are told he sat down, wept, mourned, fasted, and prayed.

After four months of beseeching God on behalf of Jerusalem, Nehemiah showed up for work with a dripping case of melancholy. The king detected Nehemiah's sadness and inquired as to its origin. Nehemiah quickly prayed to the Lord God before he answered, lest he offend the king and lose his chance to help his people—not to mention his head (gulp).

The king was open to Nehemiah's plight when he told His Majesty about Jerusalem. As a matter of fact, the king approved an extended leave of absence and provided Nehemiah with traveling papers, armed guards, and enough wood to make important repairs and improvements. Wow, what a boss!

Now, what in this fractured world of ours does all that have to do with us? Actually, plenty. For we are all called to be cupbearers—to drink deeply of life, and then to respond appropriately and even gratefully. That's not easy since life often is tainted with corruption and misery. If you're like me, you've noted folks who have endured extreme hardships with grace and you've wondered how they did it. I've tried to imagine myself in their sandals, only to be tripped up by questions: How did they survive that? How did they deal with this? How did they find a place within themselves to put that without it rupturing their faith or their spirit?

One inspiring avenue I've traipsed down is to learn from those cupbearers, people who had their life's cup filled with bitterness but who were willing to drink deeply from the cup and offer their lives as a sacrifice for others. People like Eleanor Roosevelt.

A Plucky Lady

Eleanor Roosevelt was a woman of pluck. She was a champion for those in society who had no voice— the downtrodden, the work-abused, those caught in the ugly grip of prejudice. She actively pursued reform and social work before she married Franklin, and she wasn't afraid to stand for what she believed even after Franklin became her husband and then president.

Now, many of us think we would bear our cup better, too, if we were married to the president of the United States. Yet the truth is that's not always a benefit, what with the demanding schedules, the constant separations, and the moment-by-moment scrutiny—both public and private.

Unfortunately, although the Roosevelts never divorced, their marriage was unable to hold up to the strain of the presidency. But did Eleanor let that destroy her? No!

But then, that wasn't her introduction to relational abandonment. In fact, by the time Eleanor was ten years old both of her parents had died. Several years later she was sent to Europe for her education.

Perhaps her losses were what caused Eleanor to fight valiantly for those who failed and felt like outcasts. She was quoted as saying, "No one can make you feel inferior without your consent"—a truth she probably learned at great personal expense.

In 1933 Eleanor held the first all-female press conference. In 1939 she defied segregation laws and sat between whites and blacks at the Southern Conference for Human Welfare in Birmingham, Alabama. In 1943 she toured the South Pacific to boost our soldiers' morale. Instead of becoming bitter from her life-losses, Eleanor rose up and became a crusader to make life better for others.

When, at the age of seventy-eight, she died, Adlai Stevenson, statesman and ambassador to the UN, said of her, "I have lost more than a friend—I have lost an inspiration. She would rather light candles than curse the darkness, and her glow has warmed the world."

Eleanor Roosevelt bore her cup with courage and dignity.

The Word of God teaches us how to light candles rather than curse the darkness. From creation to revelation it affords us an Alpha-and-Omega overview. It presents man's desperation and God's redemption, his offer to us of a future and a hope.

As I searched the Book of Nehemiah and began to consider Jerusalem in the midst of its devastation, I thought of our broken hearts—hearts accosted by hardships, losses, crime, failure, and other aspects of brokenness. God longs to give us new life, whether we live in Jerusalem or Jersey, and also to assist in the repairs and rebuilding of our earth-weary hearts.

If you're like me, your reaction to life is ever changing. Sometimes when I sip from the cup of my life, I taste pure nectar; other times it's more like unsweetened lemonade; and in some moments it's definitely bitterroot. And I'm aware of moments when my reaction to circumstances or to people outweighs what the situation called for (usually a sign of a heart-line fracture). I want to drink from the cup that's been given to me, but quite honestly I need h-e-l-p! If you do as well, then we're on the right road together. The Book of Nehemiah offers us ways to mend those broken hearts of ours.

Lord, intermingle the elixir of acceptance into our cups that we might drink deeply of all that you have for us. Teach us, our King, to trust what you pour into our lives, and may we bear our cups with the blazing candle of holy pride.

HEART MENDERS

What's in your cup? No, not caffeine, silly. I mean the quality of your life's content. When your cup is jostled, does it douse others in anger? Would you say you overflow with joy? Would those around you agree? Is the elixir of your life sweet or pungent? Are you willing to bear the cup you've been poured with the heart of a cheerful servant? How might you do that?

NEXT

Before we travel toward Jerusalem, I would like us to pause and consider how royal servants respond to bad news . . . the kind of news that breaks our hearts.

CHAPTER THREE

Royal Response to Really Bad News

TO DO.

Read Nehemiah 1:4–11.

I love to observe people's responses to the unexpected; you learn so much about them and their ability to handle the press of life. I also value remembering what they did or didn't do. Even strangers have served as models for me, especially when they've had a royal response.

Take, for example, Queen Elizabeth, the Queen Mother. During World War II, she refused to ship her children out of London to safety because most of her subjects weren't able to send their children away. During some of the roughest bombings, she visited the people to encourage them.

Imagine this: Sirens screamed danger as the English waited for the attacks they knew would follow. Huddled in dark air-raid shelters, they prayed their loved ones had all made it to safety. The dreaded sounds of airplane engines roared in the distance, piercing whistles streaked through the air, and then explosions sounded with such force the earth shuddered beneath their feet. The all clear finally would sound, and the people would reenter the streets of their war-torn existence. Then, through the dust and the smoke, the queen would step, dressed in a royal suit, purse over her arm, hat properly set atop her head, extending her glove-clad hands to the weary, the weak, and the wounded. Cheering them by her very presence and all she represented, the queen lifted their spirits and spurred them on to greater courage.

She was such a stalwart to England that Hitler called her "the most dangerous woman in Europe." England never forgot her bravery and her sacrifices on her subjects' behalf, and she continues to be revered. No wonder . . . no wonder.

Imagine all the power of royalty at your fingertips and then having a servant's response. How admirable.

Recently the Queen Mother celebrated her one-hundredth birthday and made a public appearance to greet England—despite bomb threats. Her courage never diminished, from facing the bombs of World War II to the threats hurled at her today. You go, girl!

Life can be startling and news appalling even for the folks who live in royal surroundings, which was true for the Queen Mother and also for the palace servant Nehemiah. Let's examine his reactions to bad news and see how he fared.

Take It In

"When I heard these words, I sat down and wept and mourned for days; and I was fasting and praying before the God of heaven" (Neh. 1:4).

When reports reached him about the continued desolation of Jerusalem, first Nehemiah sat down.

Now, I don't know about you, but often my reaction to dreadful news is to speed up. I start to sprint lickety-split in an attempt to outrun the reality or to tell everyone I know about the dilemma, hoping to find an immediate solution or at least to vent. I tell my husband and my adult children, and then I phone my closest friends. Even when I'm on the telephone I don't sit down but pace while I'm talking. (Which, I might mention, drives my family banana crackers. They're certain one day they'll find me entombed in the telephone cord.)

Author and theologian Richard Foster says, "We pant through an endless series of activities with scattered minds and noisy hearts."

Nehemiah's "sit-down" approach to trouble is so settling, so sane. (I wonder if that's why it eluded me.) And, might I mention, so spiritual. You might want to schedule a time to thumb through a Bible concordance to visit some of the verses that talk about the wisdom of "waiting" upon the Lord.

Have a Good Cry

Second, Nehemiah wept. He must have cared deeply for his homeland and people to have that kind of response to their quandary. Perhaps he had immediate family and friends in Jerusalem as well, which would certainly add to his dismay. Clearly he saw the people's hearts were so undone by their broken-down town that they couldn't rebuild it. They were a people in trouble physically and spiritually.

Tears are a powerful agent in helping to relieve pain and pressure. I'm told that, if you place a tear under a microscope, you will see toxins floating about, or doing the backstroke, or whatever toxins do for recreation besides making us sick. So tears release not only pent-up emotions but also yucky stuff.

I personally get teary at the strangest times, and sometimes when I cry for other people, I've found the first tears I shed are for them, but the rest are for me. Their predicament touches some tender or unhealed place in my own heart, giving me opportunity to spill a little more of my pain.

To suddenly feel a long-forgotten, buried pain can be scary because it goes so deep, and initially that pain can surge up with a jarring force. But tears are an important step in resolving yesterday's offenses and failures. Sarah Flower Adams must have felt the same way when she penned this line in one of her hymns: "Joys and tears alike are sent to give the soul fit nourishment."

A Time to Mourn

Third, Nehemiah mourned. Mourning is a process I would rather avoid. Mourning takes time, and I'm always in a hurry, especially to dart away from anything that brings discomfort. Yet when pain has overtaken me and I've had to slow down and step through my losses, I've found the plodding important to my emotional makeup, my mental outlook, and my spiritual understanding. But my tendency to sidestep mourning sets me up for depression, disillusionment, and disturbing doubt.

Even though grieving is a personal passage, you can experience grief relief in the midst of your pain. One way is to allow someone else to know your private feelings. For some reason putting pain into words can help us breathe more deeply. Also, allowing another person to weep with us lifts part of our heaviness.

But beware of judging someone's loyalty by how that person grieves. Just because he or she grieves differently doesn't mean the hurt isn't as great as yours. Some folks run fast and stay busy in an attempt to keep their grief at bay, but eventually it catches up.

My friend Jon was diagnosed with a terminal illness and was given six months to a year to live. He carried on with his daily routine as if the doctor had told him he had a bad cold. When family or friends tried to discuss his impending death, he changed the subject or left the room. Even his minister had no success breaking through.

Then Jon's cousin died. He had been friendly with the cousin although never close, but when Jon attended the funeral, something about being in the presence of death triggered his own reality. He began to cry until his sobs could be heard through the sanctuary. Grief can be delayed but never denied.

As a tombstone in New England reads, "It is a fearsome thing to love that which death can touch."

A Food Break

Fourth, Nehemiah fasted.

I like food—a lot! To give it up on purpose takes real effort. Even denying myself dessert feels sacrificial. Oh, I can give up, say, hot-fudge sundaes. No problem. Just don't ask me to pass up my graham crackers and milk. Yuk, you say? Well, what food(s) do you shudder at giving up? Bread? Pasta? Potatoes? Chocolate? Gummi Bears?

Everybody has his or her food weaknesses. My dad's was torn pieces of biscuit dropped in a glass and covered with buttermilk (double yuk!).

Have you noticed that denial purges the soul and liberates the spirit? I've also realized that, when I deliberately give up something to focus on something else, my concentration improves.

It reminds me of when I have an eye exam, and the doctor quizzes me on which lens I can see through best as he flips back and forth between lens choices. Fasting is like donning finely tuned spiritual spectacles that help you to see clearly.

Also, fasting can bring about a number of physical benefits from weight loss to improved taste buds to a relaxed digestive tract. You can add to that list a heightened sensitivity and discernment of the things of God, and—the finest benefit of all—a sweet exchange with the Lord. I'm not sure why we are drawn closer to God by giving up food, but perhaps when we fast we aren't thinking so much about ourselves, and our bodies aren't trying to digest the last six chocolate-chip cookies we hurriedly consumed. Then we can offer ourselves more wholeheartedly to spiritual matters. Or maybe when we sacrifice our appetites to demonstrate our hunger and thirst for God, he honors our efforts.

Prayer Time

Fifth, Nehemiah prayed. Apparently Nehemiah's fasting was to prepare him to pray. I know that we can pray anywhere at any time without fasting—or for that matter without sitting. Many a time while in full gallop I've called on the God of thunder to hear my lightning-bolt prayers. But he is also the God of quiet streams, peaceful meadows, and windless nights. Like Nehemiah, I've found value in becoming still in God's presence. Fasting

25

aids in slowing down the body's demands of us while enlivening our spirit's receptivity, which allows us to pray with a heart tilted toward heaven.

In Nehemiah's prayer he takes responsibility for his personal sin and confesses the sins of his father's house as well. I've wondered about that. Do you think some of the battles we're in today have something to do with generational sin, patterns of behavior that have been passed down from one generation to the next such as workaholics, abuse, alcoholics, rage-aholics (those addicted to their anger and willing to share it)? Just a thought. Think we should schedule a prayer session? Couldn't hurt.

Sit, weep, mourn, fast, and pray. All these verbs are truly royal verbs yet a servant's vocabulary. I would say Nehemiah's responses were every bit as royal as the Queen Mother's. In fact, I'd give them both degrees in servanthood.

Lord God of gentle breezes and quiet moments, still my noisy heart and my busy head. May I settle into your compassionate Spirit and weep for your hurting people. And may grief's season lead me into acts of sacrificial love.

HEART MENDERS

Sit

If you're not a sitter, designate a chair in your home for that purpose. Then three times a day, for five minutes each time, practice sitting quietly. No telephone in hand, no television or radio filling in the air space, just you and the stillness, making peace. Increase the time until you become comfortable with yourself, the quiet, and the Lord.

Weep

If you cry a lot, ask the Lord why. And if you hardly cry at all, ask the Lord why. Too many tears can be a sign of an open wound that needs mending; no tears can indicate we have shut off some important feelings, feelings that help us to stay compassionate and vital. We want to remain tender but not traumatized, and we want to remain open but not victimized.

I find an occasional hearty cry is a great stress reliever. And to feel another's pain deeply enough that we cry for them is scriptural as long as we don't assume responsibility for their lives—that's the Lord's job.

When was the last time you had a vigorous cry? In recent months, whom have you wept for?

Mourn

Do you feel other people's losses? How have you expressed your grief over their loss (flowers, notes, prayers, tears)? Do you feel your own losses? Or are you too busy, numb, or angry? In the last year what losses have caused you grief (a friendship, the death of a loved one, someone's trust, a job, a home, a pet)?

Fast

What are your three favorite foods to indulge in? Would you be willing to give them up for two weeks as an offering to the Lord? (Shhh, don't tell anyone but him.)

Pray

How long has it been since you knelt to pray? Try it; you'll like it (even if you, like me, need help to get back up). If you've never attempted writing your prayers, pen a few. You might be surprised what tumbles out of your heart onto the page. Singing also is a sweet addition to prayer time as well as reading Scripture aloud. (Try Psalm 100; it's a real spirit-lifter.)

NEXT
_____

Speaking of servants, wanna be one? Before responding, read on.

CHAPTER FOUR

Reconstruction Starts: Developing a Giving Heart

TO DO.

Read Nehemiah 2:1–2:8.

Surprise! The place to start mending our hearts is in helping others, in becoming a servant, of all things. I know, I know—many of us bristle at the thought of being anyone's lackey. Well, a king's, maybe, but we certainly would insist on a bulging benefits package (e.g., our own tower, moat swimming privileges, season tickets to the jousting events). Our demand-your-rights society doesn't look favorably on anything that reeks of subservience. Why, often service-oriented businesses teem with folks who act offended at having to serve customers. We live in a world that views servanthood as if it were a pair of orthopedic sandals—they might be a good choice, but no one would be caught wearing them in public. But give me a chance to make my case, okay? After all, our hearts are at stake here.

Recently I read an article that called for people to stop using housekeepers because it's a demeaning status. Of course, the fellow didn't say what those in the cleaning profession would do without paychecks, nor did he address the idea that to restore order to a home is not only an art but also an honorable service.

I wonder what advice that gentleman would have given Nehemiah, who spent his life serving others. Talk about needing to tidy up, imagine cleaning up a city that had lain in ruin for more than a hundred years! We see Nehemiah place himself repeatedly in danger that his people might know deliverance. He suffered the false accusations of political peers and their attempts to tarnish his reputation. Yet he remained faithful as he mopped up the mess the pillaging and plundering had left behind.

Even today life offers us daily prospects to grow a servant's heart, and I'm convinced servanthood is about our growth—at least it is for me. Distributing our lives wisely helps to mend our own hearts. As we give from our hearts, we receive in return a balm for our personal aches. As we meet others' needs, somehow our needs are met as well. It's a formula no one can quite figure out, but the results are consistently there. Is servanthood the whole answer for our brokenness? No, but it's a royal beginning.

And I believe we can make up our minds to be servants, even to put forth a heroic effort to change our self-consuming ways, but unless Christ is involved, our endeavors are, at best, temporary. We need him to press life-changing, grace-producing, liberating truth into the depths of our being, past our personality type and past our gene pool. Servanthood is about attitude, love, and relinquishment, and those character changes must be worked into us through a long, clumsy obedience and through the Lord's merciful intervention.

Unappealing Love

Servanthood seems to be paradoxical, as it contains conflicting elements. Elements like unappealing love. Huh?

Haven't you observed that those who royally serve others almost always are involved in rather unappealing sacrificial acts of love? Take for instance Mother Teresa, who invested her energies in helping the destitute. Her life and love were extolled by millions, but few were willing to slip into the servant habit and help her tend infectious running wounds. (Certainly not me, who doesn't like touching public doorknobs lest I be accosted by a herd of cooties.) Mother Teresa's servant's heart was attractive, but the price she paid was too severe for most of us. We tend to applaud and admire the Mother Teresas from a safe and sanitary distance.

My friend Shirley Valade is a servant, a truly royal servant. For three years she was the main caregiver for her in-laws until both died. They required constant attention and backbreaking effort to see to their needs. She fed them, bathed them, diapered them, and doctored them with tender mercies until they took their last breaths. Her husband told me that Shirley did more for his mom than most folks would do for their own moms. Today Shirley is often bed-bound by rheumatoid arthritis, and her husband generously and tenderly cares for her. Servanthood must run in their family.

I'll never be a Mother Teresa in Calcutta, and I'll never be called on to care for my in-laws (they are both deceased). But I also know God expects me to be more considerate and accommodating to others than I am. I realize I need to give away, give in, and give up my so-called rights more often than I do.

Deliberate Acts of Kindness

In fact, I wonder how many times a day I miss servant opportunities in which I could extend myself in gracious ways. I could allow someone to go ahead of me at the checkout lane, hold my silence when someone is rude or wrong, and give up indulgences for myself, choosing instead to donate to someone who has much less. I'm asked to remember the afflicted, the hurting, the poor, the imprisoned, and the lost of this world.

We can do that with funds, visits, cards, prayers, baskets, or all of the aforementioned. And let's not forget to refresh the Mother Teresas and the Shirleys of this world. Serving the servants sounds right to me.

But I think our first servant call, before we attempt

to take on our neighborhoods or communities, is to the folks who live in our homes. Remember that servanthood isn't indulging people's weaknesses but sacrificially supporting their efforts to make wise and healthy choices. I say that lest we have some indulgent parents or mates who keep rescuing their family members from the important lessons of living with the consequences of their choices. Often those consequences contain the components that will bring about the lasting changes we have prayed for.

An Ear to Heaven

Recently I read of a large, awkward, young man who joined a monastery hoping to be cured of his clumsiness through regimented self-denial. Instead, as he sought the Lord for change, he was overtaken by a growing awareness of God's acceptance and love of him just the way he was. The Lord's encompassing presence and the man's mended heart can be heard in his letters, better known to us as *The Practice of the Presence of God* by Brother Lawrence.

Brother Lawrence, a monastery cook, was sought out by the scholarly not for his sauces but for his sense, his God-sense. This monk from the order of the Carmelites Dechausses lived in the clatter of his kitchen environment with a constant ear open to heaven. Servanthood for this lumbering brother was not an effort but a pleasure, not degrading but a privilege.

I confess I prefer to be served rather than to serve, especially at mealtime. The clatter in my kitchen has too often been from my grumbling as I lumber between my sink and stove. I don't find cooking easy, and seldom do I receive applause for my clumsy culinary efforts. I think servanthood must be similar in that it's unnatural for most of us and often, if our sacrifices go unnoticed, we are left stewing in our own sauce.

When our service is out of a need to seek others' approval (I'm guilty), our self-serving efforts do little more than seep between the cracks of this broken world.

So do we join a monastery, book a flight to Calcutta, or sign up for a nursing course to become a royal servant? Perhaps, although more than likely most of us will make our servant contributions right where we are among those we already know. We might offer a listening ear to a troubled friend, allowing him or her to talk out frustrations without offering advice; compassionately dry a child's tears; joyfully assist an elderly person with errands; or give up our right to the last word in a heated squabble.

I think we will find more of what it means to be a royal servant as we make our way to Jerusalem with Nehemiah and begin to rebuild. But first, before we tread down that road, I'd like to show you something I discovered in my studies. I was delighted to see parallels between two royal servants, Christ and Nehemiah.

For instance, because of Nehemiah's position in the palace, scholars believe he was from a line of either priests or princes. Christ is both our High Priest and our Prince of Peace. And yet both wholeheartedly served others. What a royal response!

Nehemiah left the castle's comforts to join his

people in their poverty. Christ left the riches of heaven to join us in our poverty. Servanthood often involves leaving a comfortable place and going somewhere we might not choose.

Nehemiah served his people as the governor of Jerusalem. Scripture says that the government rests on our Lord's shoulders. Servanthood is taking on responsibility for helping others as well as ourselves.

Nehemiah walked through Jerusalem's ruins and designed a plan of restoration. Christ walks through our hearts' ruins with a plan for our restoration and our well-being. A servant's plans include the welfare of others.

Nehemiah was the king's cupbearer. Jesus was the cupbearer on our behalf, drinking the poisonous cup of our sin that we might live forever.

Their example of dignified, humble serving encourages us to focus on giving of ourselves to others and to God as a path that leads to a mended heart. It's a mystery how, when I help someone else, it helps me, but I know it to be true. And when I seek to alleviate the pain in another's heart, it eases my pain.

I experienced the reality of this mystery when I went through the tragic loss of a friend by suicide. I was at the house when the body was found and when the family was told of their loss. I was involved in providing emotional support to the grieving family and was feeling the devastating loss of my friend while I wondered if I could have done something to prevent it.

Then I was asked to do the eulogy. I didn't feel I had the reserves to speak at the funeral, but after praying, I felt I needed to do it.

So with a trembling jaw, shaking hands, and a

heavy heart, I made my way to the front of the sanctuary to console the people in attendance. This act ministered to my own needs in ways I never would have guessed. My feeble attempt to serve the family ended up becoming a solace to me and a balm to my hurt heart. I don't understand the mystery of God's ways, but he uses his people as servants to help make them whole—including the person doing the serving.

Lord, teach me not to be aggressive and defensive in this already self-absorbed world. Help me not to be afraid of my weakness and my inadequacy to be your servant. I want to be a faithful agent of your mercy, beginning in small ways so that, with your help, I can grow into orthopedic sandals and take servanthood on the road. Amen.

HEART MENDERS

How do you serve others? Do you have the internal grace to acquiesce to family members, coworkers, and friends? List three ways that you will purpose to serve someone this week.

NEXT

Let's head to Jerusalem. Did you pack? It's okay; servants never require a great deal.

CHAPTER FIVE

Enemy Talk:
Five Lies to Do You In

TO DO.

Read Nehemiah 4:1–3

In my neighborhood, when I was a youngster, we had a singsong catchphrase we would taunt each other with when we didn't like what another kid was saying: "Liar, liar, pants on fire. . . ." Not a very sweet sentiment yet a seemingly apt retort when we refer to Satan, old hot britches himself, who specializes in deceit. His lies lead us into heartbreak every time we believe him.

As I've mentioned before, during my twenties I struggled with panic attacks and eventually became a prisoner in my home, afraid of the outside world. My attacks were a gripping series of physical symptoms fueled by my frail emotions. I felt a tightening in my chest and as if I wouldn't be able to take another breath. My eyes would dilate. I would experience tremors, racing thoughts, and panic that my existence was threatened. Many people also suffer from sweats and heart palpitations when they have panic attacks.

While the attacks would only last for minutes, the resulting fear clung to me like Velcro. I would retreat to the safest place I could find, which was close to my husband or my mom. I especially wanted to be at home or at my mother's house. Not that I felt safe in either place—I just felt *safer*.

I depended on the comforting words of my medical doctor and the medication he prescribed (tranquilizers). Of course, the tranquilizers actually complicated my struggle because they were ineffective and potentially addicting.

Caffeine and nicotine were also a part of my "support" system. Each day I drank ten pots (yes, folks, that's pots) of coffee, smoked two packs of cigarettes, and popped tranquilizers—and had panic attacks. Well, isn't that a surprise. I realize today that so much stimuli would have caused anyone added stress.

One of the reasons my anxiety had such a grip on my life was that I had embraced a package of lies. When a panic attack would flare, Satan would shriek, "Your mind will surely snap! You won't survive this time! You're going to die!"

Even though I did survive the panic, my mind did hold together, and I didn't die, I bought into his intimidation and treachery every time, which only increased my struggles' intensity and duration. Now, you would think if a person had a thousand panic attacks and she never keeled over, she would realize the menacing threats were faulty. But Satan is like a fledgling bugler who plays one note over and over again to try to distract and deafen us to the truth—to Christ's sweet, liberating melody. It took me time to tune out the bugle call and to enter into the Shepherd's sweet songs, his lyrical pieces that brought comfort to my battered mind and heart.

I remember one Sunday when, during my recovery from agoraphobia, my anxiety level began to soar as I sat in church. My first thought was to flee, but just then the congregation began to sing, "Turn your eyes upon Jesus, look full in his wonderful face, and the things of earth will grow strangely dim in the light of his glory and grace."[1] Those words poured over me like a balm, the tension in my body began to ease, my ricocheting heart slowed down, and my scampering thoughts settled.

Our Traveling Companion

Satan's trademarks are lies and destruction, but Christ's hallmarks are love and redemption. Satan can't mangle anything that Christ can't set anew. Scripture comforts us with this truth: "Greater is He [Christ] who is in you than he [Satan] who is in the world" (1 John 4:4). My ruffled spirit is soothed to know Christ is within me, and therefore I can't go anywhere that he won't be there with me.

Which is a good thing because, by my nature, I'm given to predicaments. I travel an average of twenty-five to thirty weekends a year, which should mean I'm a pro. But recently I arrived in a city and realized I didn't know what hotel I was booked in. I called almost every hotel in the city with this telltale question: "Do I live there?"

I have at other times found myself at odds with cabdrivers who felt led, while the meter ticked, to tour their metropolis before depositing me at my destination. And at times I've felt intimidated by an unfamiliar setting in which I'm uncertain of my safety. Often hotel guards will warn me not to walk in certain areas and not to go out once it's dark.

I'm grateful for a Savior who is willing to go on the road (and doesn't leave his meter running), for he walks before us, behind us, beside us, and dwells within us. Jesus is a way-finder, a friend-maker, and a dispeller of fear.

Satan the fear-giver has honked his bugle in the face of humanity for eons, and he continues to drone on with the same discordant sounds from his limited repertoire. For instance, when Nehemiah made his way to Jerusalem to rebuild the walls, word spread of his intentions. That's when the enemy reached for his rusty horn. You can hear the blaring lies from the mouths of Nehemiah's local enemies, Sanballat and Tobiah. These men were governors of surrounding areas, which suggests their actions were politically motivated, especially since rebuilding the city could mean it would become a new center of influence, decreasing their power. Listen in:

> Now it came about that when Sanballat heard that we were rebuilding the wall, he became furious and very angry and mocked the Jews. And he spoke in the presence of his brothers and the wealthy men of Samaria and said, "What are these feeble Jews doing? Are they going to restore it for themselves? Can they offer sacrifices? Can they finish in a day? Can they revive the stones from the dusty rubble even the burned ones?" (Neh. 4:1–2)

We're immediately alerted to the enemy's rage and taunting personality. His beguiling questions, meant to undermine Nehemiah's identity, motives, credentials, sanity, and future, hang in the air like arrows stuck in a bull's-eye. Satan shoots these same questions in our direction during hard times, new challenges, and vulnerable moments, times when our guard is down, when our walls need repair, and our hearts' gates are left ajar. Oh, the statements might sound a tad different today, but they certainly are aimed to hit the target with the same accuracy meant for Nehemiah. Therefore, we would be wise to listen in to the lies the trumpeter played for Nehemiah. That will help to prepare our hearts to respond in a way that avoids more damage and instead moves us toward healing our wounds.

Lie #1:
"*What Are These Feeble Jews Doing?*"

Can you hear Satan hiss to you, "Who do you think you are?" The enemy's insinuation was that Nehemiah was only a cupbearer, a paltry servant, so what made him think he could take on such a daunting task. Even if he united a few, feeble Jews, how could they, with their world so broken, their people so scattered, and their walls so damaged, ever succeed? Yes, Satan loves to blast away at our personal credentials, even our heritage, and certainly our vulnerability.

NEHEMIAH'S RESPONSE

What heartens me in the Book of Nehemiah is that God chose to use a humble cupbearer, not a noted architect, to rebuild the city. Nehemiah must have been quite aware of his lack of credentials but more aware of his miraculous God. When Nehemiah presented his résumé to the people, this is what he said: "I told them how the hand of my God had been favorable to me" (Neh. 2:18*a*). That seemed to be just what the people had been waiting for, a man sent by Jehovah. As a result, God's scattered people did unite rather than yell, "Every man for himself." And their walls were reconstructed, not left in heaps of rubble. Yeah, team!

Many times when I travel to speak, the thought crosses my mind, *Patsy, who are you to tell anyone how to live when you are so feeble?* Perhaps (probably) I've quarreled with my husband that week without resolution. Or I've spoken unkindly to a salesclerk, or I've spent the day whining, and now I'm supposed to stand before others and speak of victory. I can't tell you how many times I've had to fall on my face before the Lord and ask for his forgiveness as well as to be reminded by his Spirit that Jesus is the ultimate qualifier. Not what I do or don't do, but who he is. Yeah, God!

GOD'S ANSWER

Conviction is an important part of our spiritual lives, and when the Holy Spirit speaks to us, he does so with an inner urging, a wooing to come closer to Christ through confession and forgiveness. The Holy Spirit presses into our wounded hearts the life-giving truth of our value to the Lord and in the Lord. We're reassured that the God of the heavens knows us intimately and loves us deeply. He knows the number of hairs on our heads, and if that bit of changing trivia (check your hairbrush) is important to him, how much more must our struggles and heartaches touch him. The Spirit's work of lifting up Christ, like a holy symphony, leaves a song—no, make that a concert—in our hearts.

In contrast, our archenemy screeches defamatory statements, like fingernails on a chalkboard, in an attempt to distract us from our calling and to smudge our value. Oh, how he relishes hitting the identity note, an area most of us struggle with already without the help of his sick recitals. His work, like a cacophony, leaves us jarred.

We need to be sensitive to God's nudges, for he will enable us to guard our minds against our adversary's screaming tactics when he tries his best to bulldoze or skulk his way in on our feebleness. How wonderful that we serve a God who formed us and therefore understands our frailty and susceptibility yet has grace-filled plans for us. He is an ever-present God who promises to lead and guide us all the days of our lives. He will never abandon us.

Years ago a wise woman instructed me to keep short accounts with the Lord as a path to grow in God's ways. By bringing my sins before him on a regular basis, I stayed current in my relationship with him, not allowing offenses to mount up inside me. Then, as I consistently sought the Lord for counsel through his Word, prayer, confession, and fellowship, I was free to become more familiar with the sound of his nurturing voice, which protected me from disparaging influences like the adversary's screeches. My friend's advice has held me in good spiritual stead.

Lie #2:
"Are They Going to Restore It for Themselves?"

This time intimidation is the head-wagger's weapon as he throws low blows, questioning our motives: "Why are you *really* doing this?"

Have you ever had someone question your motives when you were doing something you meant for good? And the more you tried to defend yourself the guiltier you looked and the worse you felt, until finally even you began to doubt yourself?

I guess that's why Scripture tells us the Lord will be the one to judge our motives. Until then, beware of the guilt-giver, who will try to create inner chaos with his finger-pointing and *tsking*. *Tsking?* Yep, you know, tsk, tsk, tsk. That shaming sound that's usually accompanied with head shaking, low-cast eyes, and a judgmental spirit. Nothing, my friend, is as bleak as shame.

NEHEMIAH'S RESPONSE

Obviously Nehemiah had no doubt as to why he was rebuilding the wall. When his motives were questioned, he maintained his focus on the work before him and encouraged his people to do the same. That's why his response to the political naysayers was, "I answered them and said to them, 'The God of heaven will give us success; therefore we His servants will arise and build, but you have no portion, right, or memorial in Jerusalem'" (Neh. 2:20). The same is true for our enemy; Satan has no portion, right, or commemorative locale in God's kingdom.

GOD'S ANSWER

I'm grateful Jesus the Grace-Giver extends the amazing gift of grace even when our motives are less than honorable. Remember the New Testament prostitute? She didn't seek out Jesus but was thrown into his presence guilty as charged. She was caught in the act of adultery, encircled by eyewitnesses, dragged into Christ's holy presence by her shaming accusers with her death sentence imminent. The Savior responds by writing in the dust of the earth her reprieve. The enemy must have cringed that day as the Lord released her from her accusers and liberated her from her crimson shame. Christ instructed her to "go, and sin no more" (John 8:11 KJV). Nothing, my friend, is as luminous as grace.

If we could have heard her heart's prayer that day, I wonder if it would have sounded something like this: "Oh, gracious Lord, you have picked me up out of the dirt of my life and given me a clean heart. It has been so long since anything about me has been clean, and so long since I've been able to lift my head and look other people in the eye. Today I met your gaze, and I shall never be the same. I want to climb the distant mountain and shout to the morning sun what you have done."

Lie #3:
"Can They Offer Sacrifices?"

No wonder our opponent is called the deceiver; he never seems to miss an opportunity to toss in his plug nickel. This time it's to intone, "With all the blunders you've made, you're going to sacrifice to God?" Satan insists we have no right to approach God's throne; Satan condemns us by bringing up our failures.

The citizens of Jerusalem certainly were vulnerable to such accusations. They had failed to rebuild their city and to deal with their past sins (Neh. 1:6–7). But even as the wall was being rebuilt, problems arose within the city. Poverty-stricken people came to Nehemiah complaining about fellow Jews' usury that forced those who were financially strapped to sell their children into bondage.

NEHEMIAH'S RESPONSE

Nehemiah "consulted" with himself and "contended" with the nobles, telling them, "The thing which you are doing is not good; should you not walk in the fear of our God . . . ?" (Neh. 5:9). But rather than carping on their misbehavior, he turned his attention to what was an appropriate response. He ordered them to give back the fields, the vineyards, the olive groves, and the homes that had been confiscated.

The nobles responded to this call for repentance and restitution, and the city, which had become divided among itself, was brought back together as Nehemiah concentrated on making the situation right. I'm impressed that he didn't whip them with their misdeeds but led them into acts of integrity, which helped to solidify their character and to unite their community.

As I consider Satan's lie that we are undeserving, I think about Chuck Colson and what he must have endured in his beginning walk with Christ. Right in the middle of national scandal, this aide to former president Richard Nixon, also known as the White House Hatchet Man, announced his conversion to Christianity. The enemy must have had a heyday in his attempt to condemn Chuck and to keep him under his circumstances. And because of his position and the Watergate melee, Chuck found himself under heavy scrutiny by the general public. Folks wondered if his so-called "repentance" was just an effort to divert attention from his guilt. Only time could prove the legitimacy of his encounter with Christ.

Chuck spent seven months in prison and now has spent twenty-five years in the prison ministry he started; it has become one of the largest volunteer organizations in the world. Chuck's integrity and his faithful outreach to prisoners, their families, and their victims have won him the respect of many. Instead of living under condemnation, his faith has brought him above reproach.

GOD'S ANSWER

We're invited, instructed, encouraged to approach the throne of grace with boldness, with the confidence that Christ, who promised acceptance, will receive us—yes, even at our worst. It took me a while to understand I was forgiven and therefore acceptable to Christ despite my addictions, failures, and insecurity. I had gone forward in church to pray at the altar many times, hoping my repeated pleas for forgiveness would be heard. I desperately felt the need for Christ to transform my wreck of a life. Then it slowly dawned on me that Christ was faithful and therefore I was clean before the Lord. My flawed condition, my guilt, and the enemy's lies had distorted my understanding of God's acceptance. Nothing deters the enemy like a clean heart and a clear conscience . . . just ask the prostitute, or Chuck Colson, or me.

Lie #4:
"Can They Finish in a Day?"

Amid humiliating guffaws the liar snarls, "Are you out of your mind?"

For years the rubber bands of my emotions were pulled so taut I was convinced I was one yank short of the funny farm—and I wasn't laughing. My fearful thoughts kept me stumbling about emotionally. The enemy, who is the "prince of the power of the air" (Eph. 2:2), uses his transmitting influence to divert us mentally. He hopes that, if he can persuade us to think his way, we will lose ours.

Thoughts become the food our emotions feed on, which means if we gorge on the enemy's menu of lies, we will clamor in the darkness, lost, frightened, and forgotten. Whereas, when we feast on the Lord's thoughts, we will mature, be strengthened, stabilize, and have a sane evaluation of our worth.

NEHEMIAH'S RESPONSE

Imagine how Nehemiah felt as he faced building a wall that had been turned into rubble 150 years before. Yet, undaunted by the enemy's whispers that he was out of his mind to even try, Nehemiah managed to complete the wall in fifty-two days. That's days, not weeks or months or years, folks. Even while the governors of surrounding communities were sending taunting messages, the rows of bricks were encircling the city. Yeah, Nehemiah!

GOD'S ANSWER

Like Nehemiah, we can respond to Satan's jibe, "Are you out of your mind?" by recognizing that we don't have to give him the time of day. We can allow our minds to become factories of fear by repeating the scary lies of the enemy to ourselves. Or our minds can become fountains of faith by recalling Scripture.

One of the verses that have helped me to maintain my sanity is 2 Timothy 1:7, "For God hath not given us the spirit of fear; but of power, and of love, and of a sound mind" (KJV). According to this verse, fear leaves us feeling powerless, unloved, and mentally fragile. To combat this, God extends to us his love, his power, and his sound mind. In my research on a sound mind, which has continued over the past thirty years, I've learned that the word translated "sound mind" in our Bibles is defined as "having a proper restraint on all passions and desires." I found that not only convicting, but it also has become my life desire.

Feeding my mind by mentally dining on even one uplifting book can elevate my thoughts and boost my spirit. And when I make a steady diet of healthy materials, my mind is in a more wholesome place. As a Hebrew saying wisely counsels us, "Hold a book in your hand and you're a pilgrim at the gate of a new city."

I try to keep stacks of good literature at my fingertips—poetry, biographies, devotionals and, of course, the Scriptures. Scripture, full of liberating, steadying, deepening counsel, prepares us to detect the deceiver's discrepancies when he attempts to persuade us that our minds won't hold up. The Bible encourages us to gird up our minds—in other words, to make them battle-ready with the truth. And don't miss Scripture's eloquent poetry, gripping biographies, and unending banquets of devotional thoughts.

Lie #5:
"Can They Revive the Stones from the Dusty Rubble, Even the Burned Ones?"

This lie reeks with sarcasm as Satan bellows, "It can't be done! It's hopeless and so are you!"

My mom could have despaired on any number of occasions as she prayed for her family to know Jesus. My brother, sister, and I weren't just reluctant in our spiritual interests; we were out and out rebellious. Defying her authority and denying God's, we each went our own headstrong way. And I'm sure, when our behavior was the most despicable, Mom's heart sank as the intimidator spewed his bleakness in her direction. Yet, despite his trickery and treachery, Mom held high her faith in the God of the Impossible and prayed for more than twenty-five years, until each member of her family came to Christ. The last member was my dad, who invited Christ into his heart days before his death. It was a long haul for Mom, but her hope was birthed and nurtured in the truth that the Lord longs for all to be drawn to him.

NEHEMIAH'S RESPONSE

When Nehemiah surveyed the crumpled wall, I wonder what went through his mind. I'm sure the treacherous one tried to dissuade him from rebuilding

Jerusalem; yet obviously Nehemiah wasn't buying into Satan's diversionary tactics.

Governor Tobiah, archenemy #2 for Nehemiah, sarcastically told the influential men of the area, "Even what they are building—if a fox should jump on it, he would break their stone wall down!" (Neh. 4:3). A real comedian, considering that foxes tend to travel alone, are made up mostly of fur, and are small, insignificant beasts to begin with.

Tobiah was spreading the fib that the wall was pretty close to falling down of its own accord; his biting sarcasm was meant to undermine and ridicule the efforts of God's people.

And it worked because lies and fears breed hopelessness. Nehemiah notes in his prayer that the enemy had demoralized the builders (Neh. 4:5). They were beginning to believe the lie that their efforts were wasted; the work was too great, and the enemies too threatening. Interestingly enough, in the following verse, we see that the builders are once again making progress.

What made the difference? The liberating key phrase "for the people had a mind to work." The workers went from demoralization to rededication by refusing the lie and disciplining their thoughts. A mind set in God's direction exudes strength. It truly is a sound mind, not filled with fear but with an awareness of God's love and power.

When Jerusalem's enemies saw that the work continued, they conspired together to cause a disturbance by spreading rumors throughout Judah that the builders' strength was failing and that they were knee-deep in rubbish (Neh. 4:10). Oh, how the enemy longs to keep us focused on our lives' debris lest we be heartened by our progress. A sense of hopelessness grows when we keep our eyes on the size of the tasks measured against our frailty and weakness.

Several years ago, our youngest son, Jason, signed up to play baseball with the other grade-school kids. My husband and I became his biggest cheerleaders, but by the fourth game we saw our work was cut out for us. Jason wouldn't swing the bat. It was as if Velcro kept it stuck to his shoulder. Time after time he would march up to the plate, lean slightly forward, and watch the balls swish by. We encouraged him to swing, we practiced swinging with him, and we cheered for him if we thought he was even contemplating swinging. But, alas, the boy would not move his bat. We told him he didn't have to hit the ball, but please take a swing.

At the end of the season, when awards were handed out, Jason received the trophy for being on base more than any other player on his team. You see, the only thing worse than Jason's batting average was the opposing pitchers' abilities to throw strikes.

If I could return to the good old days, when my youngster was playing baseball, you would hear a different cheer emanating from the stands. I wouldn't focus on what was too hard for Jason to risk: instead I'd congratulate him on perfect attendance, his ability to get along with his teammates, and his willingness to step up to the plate repeatedly. I'd look at what he could do, not what he couldn't.

And that's how Nehemiah encouraged his people, not wanting them to focus on how much work lay before them but on how much they already had done (the wall was halfway up), that God was with them, and that they would provide emotional and physical support for each other.

GOD'S ANSWER

The psalmist said, "He delivered me from all my fears." The word *delivered* means "to show a way out." Rats, I was hoping for a white knight to swoop in, pull me onto his steed, and gallop away from my hopeless-looking situation. But no, God apparently prepares a way out of our futility but expects us to find the exit. Don't misunderstand—we aren't mice in a maze, but we will need to rise up and take some responsibility. We will need to have "a mind to work."

Another Day, More Lies

When Nehemiah and the people made measurable progress in the rebuilding, his enemies became desperate and therefore more aggressive in their campaign of character, political, and personal assassination. They invited Nehemiah to join them for a confab on the plain of Ono.

And "Oh, no," was the response Nehemiah gave them. In fact, he said, "I am doing a great work and I cannot come down. Why should the work stop while I leave it and come down to you?" (Neh. 6:3).

Nehemiah kept insisting that to join them would create a downward spiral for him. Well, after they sent the message four times, the enemies then tried a new strategy, one of slander.

> It is reported among the nations, and Gashmu says, that you and the Jews are planning to rebel; therefore you are rebuilding the wall. And you are to be their king, according to these reports. And you have also appointed prophets to proclaim in Jerusalem concerning you, "A king is in Judah!" And now it will be reported to the king according to these reports. So come now, let us take counsel together. (Neh. 6:6–7)

What scoundrels! In an attempt to entice Nehemiah, his enemies cleverly devised statements they hoped would cause Nehemiah to bolt away from his people's protection to defend his reputation. But Nehemiah wasn't so full of himself that he needed to run around protecting his public persona, and he was wise enough to recognize the faultiness of the information. Listen to Nehemiah's retort: "Such things as you are saying have not been done, but you are inventing them in your own mind" (Neh. 6:8). Nehemiah was so settled in who he was, why he was in Jerusalem, and whom he was doing the rebuilding for that nothing was going to deter him. What focus, what commitment!

Recently I saw a television presentation on a young woman dubbed "The Butterfly." Her fluttering nickname came about as she positioned herself more than two hundred feet in the air on a small, tarp-covered platform in a mammoth redwood tree. There, poised like a monarch on a cattail, Butterfly gained a large audience. Some were appreciative. Some were angry. You see, Butterfly was a tree-sitter. She was taking a towering stand against the cutting down of the ancient trees. Some applauded her efforts and supported her by bringing in supplies. But others despised the negative press she was garnering against those who cut down the trees. Her enemies hurled insults while her supporters heaped praise on this lofty lady.

Regardless of how one might feel about her tree-saving efforts, even her enemies were stunned at her tenacity. For Butterfly remained on her small wooden perch for more than two years. Yes, two years. Nothing deterred her from seeing her calling through. And "through" is what she experienced as she endured whipping storms, heat, restricted movement, and times of isolation. Her adverse situation seemed to deepen her resolve. None of her enemies' aggressive and demeaning ploys to end her tree living would bring her down, even though she was in an exceedingly vulnerable place.

And so are we. Insinuation, intimidation, condemnation, humiliation, accusation, and assassination make up the threatening arsenal set against us. Are we victims without recourse to these heartbreaking lies? Praise God, we aren't! The Nehemiahs, the

Chuck Colsons, and the praying moms of this world give us hope that we don't have to believe Johnny One-Note, but that we can, instead, tune our hearts into Jesus' symphony of grace and love, enabling us to be valiant in the face of adversity.

Dear Lord, in this frenetic world of distractions help us to turn our eyes upon you.

HEART MENDERS

Lie #1
When do you struggle with feelings of unworthiness? What thoughts crowd your mind? Do you stay current with the Lord through prayer and confession? How do you feel afterward? Valued? Loved?

Lie #2
Has anyone shamed you with his or her words? Tone? Eyes? Behavior? Have you shamed anyone? Define *grace*. How have you been the recipient of grace? Who extended it?

Lie #3
What failures haunt you and leave you with the fear you can't be loved by God? What task might you undertake to make restitution for a past failure and to help release you from that shortcoming?

Lie #4

Is your mind a factory of fear or a fountain of faith? In what ways have you grown emotionally and spiritually in the past year? List three areas that have been strengthened in the past year. What kind of brainfood (thoughts) are you ruminating on?

Lie #5

List three hopeless thoughts you find difficult to escape. In what ways is God greater than circumstances?

Other Lies

Who has taken potshots at your reputation? What can you do to stand firm?

NEXT

_____

I have a confession to make . . .

CHAPTER SIX

By the Way . . .

Thinking of the lies that were flung at Nehemiah in the last chapter, I'm reminded that enemies aren't the only ones who lie to us. Sometimes we lie to ourselves. For me, at times the lies are small ones such as pretending I haven't gained weight even when I need help to button my britches. Or bigger ones such as when I try to convince myself that some sarcastic comment of mine that caused someone to wince wasn't a big deal. And sometimes, yes, sometimes I've been guilty of a whopper.

The good thing is that I can bring my darkened heart to Christ and be forgiven and liberated from my dishonest, self-protective tendencies. We're told that, if we confess, Christ forgives.

Undercover Lies

But the unknown lies, the ones that have been woven into our character through damage, pain, and misinformation, are the most insidious to deal with. They rattle around in our behavior, seek refuge in our personalities, hide in our opinions, even burrow into our spirituality, and blind us to the truth.

My husband, Les, grew up in a violent home. His raging father often woke the family in a tirade. The six children never knew where his wrath would fall, and many nights they lay trembling as they heard their mother's cries while she bore the brunt of his fury. That was more than forty years ago (Les's dad died when Les was sixteen), and yet to this day, when Les unexpectedly is awakened, he will flail with fright. Once he is conscious and realizes his surroundings, he's fine.

Les's father's behavior convinced Les he wasn't safe as a child, which was true. But the enemy told Les he would never be safe. Satan waits for vulnerable moments to breathe lies into a child's broken trust.

Lie Replacement

How do we participate in the mending of our hearts so they won't believe the lies anymore? First, we ask the Holy Spirit, who has promised to guide and lead us into all truth, to help us spot the lies we live by.

Then, when they are revealed, we replace them with the truth.

An insensitive family that used sarcastic humor to release anger raised a foster child, Greta, in an emotionally caustic environment. Often the message she received under the guise of humor was that she wasn't very bright or attractive. Feeling like an odd duck anyway, Greta was a prime candidate to have her heart seeded with deception. Even though she developed into an attractive adult, she was painfully shy and chose to work out of her home rather than risk the stress a workplace and relationships would bring.

One Sunday, after several invitations from a neighbor and in an attempt to dodge the haunting loneliness that stalked her, Greta attended a local church. There she heard about Christ and his longing to fill her aching heart. She embraced his offer and began to grow in her understanding of her neediness and of God's lavish provisions. Christ became her counselor, the Holy Spirit her comforter. In time she replaced the lies regarding her intelligence and her physical appearance, as she realized she was valued and loved in the Lord. But to her surprise, Greta learned something else needed to change, and that was the vows she had made as a result of the lies.

Protective Promises

Vows can be wonderful, such as the precious ones we make on our wedding day, the promise we make to a child, or the commitment we make to God. But, as in most things taken to an extreme, even a vow can work against us. Vows can be self-protective promises we make in our hearts to combat the lies and the painful treatment we endure when we're young. Vows give the child an inner voice that helps him or her to survive, but those same vows become counterproductive as adults.

In Greta's case, she vowed she would keep her distance from all grown-ups because they inflicted pain, which prevented her as an adult from meaningful friendships. Gradually, as she realized why she had created her vow, she faced her fears and developed nurturing relationships, ones in which she could love and be loved.

My friend Jan Frank is a counselor and author who specializes in sexual abuse and marriage issues. She shared with me that when a child makes a heart vow that isn't dealt with as an adult, the vow becomes bondage, and the bondage a generational curse. A generational curse occurs when our behavior becomes a family pattern reproduced by example over and over again.

Lori, a friend who was sexually abused by her father, was taught that her role was to take care of him. She grew up believing the lie that at all costs to herself she should please others. This behavior won her many friends but cost her huge chunks of her identity. After unraveling the memories of her abuse and step-by-step walking and working toward healing, replacing the lie with the truth, she gradually came into her own. She began to give herself permission to disagree with others and even to disappoint them if what was being asked of her was inappropriate.

Yet Lori saw one day how this unreasonable pattern was being passed on. She found her young son sitting at the bottom of their stairwell crying. When she asked him what was wrong, he tearfully told her, "If I go upstairs to be with Dad, I'm afraid you'll be sad. But if I stay down here with you, I'm afraid Dad might be unhappy."

Lori was stunned to realize her little boy was following in her footsteps, attempting to make everyone happy. She was sobered, for she, like us, wanted only the best for her family. So we need to learn to deal honestly with our history, if we are to improve the quality of our futures and if we are to find the heart-mending we know we need.

For me, the truth is I fear that as the Lord pulls threads out of the tapestry of my life, I'll unravel. Yet I've grown weary of not moving past certain unhealthy behaviors, and I long for change. Growth feels risky because it always costs something. And I have yet to see it go on sale. Honestly, sometimes I grow weary of my same old self and long for more of Christ . . . what about you?

Remember . . .

Lies strangle trust. They squelch love. Lies stunt growth. And gnarl souls. Lies seize prisoners. They cripple identity. Lies deplete us. And they infect others.

Whereas . . .
Truth liberates. And strengthens. Truth builds.
And stabilizes. Truth nurtures. And heals. Truth
endures. And blesses. And blesses. And blesses.

*Lord, inspect my inner life. I don't trust myself to do
it lest I become lost in my own darkness. Illuminate
the truth . . . and may I be wise enough to walk in
it. Amen.*

HEART MENDERS

What changes would you need to institute to be
willing to have the Lord reveal any vows you made as
a child? Does part of your heart always feel sad? Who
is a wise, objective person you could talk to about
your feelings?

NEXT

Let's take a look at the Lord's defense plan for giving
us a secure future and an eternal hope.

CHAPTER SEVEN

Ready, Aim . . . :
Six Weapons to Defend Yourself

TO DO.

Read Nehemiah 4:4–23.

I once gave a girl a bloody nose when, much to my horror and hers, I socked her a good one. I don't remember why I popped her, but the gush of blood convinced me never to do it again.

Another time, as an adult, night noises and our barking dog lit my fear, which had a short fuse, and I went in search of a weapon. I settled on long hose sections off our Kirby vacuum cleaner. Don't ask me why; maybe I thought I could suck the bad guy into the dirt bag. The hose ultimately was ineffective since it's hard to vacuum up one's imagination.

Obviously I've never been a good candidate for the armed forces, but life has taught me I'd better be prepared because the enemy fights down and dirty, and he's not beyond using others to accomplish his foul deeds. We need good defenses and to understand the enemy's tactics, if we're to guard our fragile hearts.

As we mentioned in Chapter five, Satan is the father of falsehood, and lies are both his language and main artillery, as he takes regular potshots at us. Just ask Nehemiah, who was constantly pummeled with attacks. Or ask my friend Joseph.

Old Testament Joseph, seared by flames of deception, was sold into captivity by his resentful brothers, thrown into prison by a conniving woman, and forgotten behind bars by a self-consumed fellow prisoner. Now that, folks, is enough to make anyone reach for a bottle of antacid. Why, I've wanted to cause a revolt when someone has beaten me to a parking space or dillydallied through an intersection. Yet, despite Joseph's slander-riddled circumstances, he eventually rose to become the second most powerful leader in Egypt. Family rejection, a raging female, a thwarted friendship, and years in prison—that's tough curriculum for any position, even for one in a palace.

When Joseph was, years later, reunited with his brothers, he cautiously tested their honesty before he revealed his identity. Who could blame him? The years had taught him much about the importance of guarding his heart and detecting a lie.

We note from Joseph's experience that Satan's quiver is crowded with arrows of jealousy, lust, and selfishness. If we are to stave off his attacks, we need to be astute to his deceit—so let's take a closer look.

Designer Lies

If only lies were neon and wired with shrill sirens to warn us of their combustible content. But lies aren't always obvious; in fact, they often dress up in designer originals, enticing our susceptibilities, fitting comfortably into our brokenness. And those who are dishonest aren't always flaming enemies. Sometimes, as was Joseph's case, they are our trusted friends, family, and mentors. They haven't necessarily meant to be deceivers, but their naïveté, damage, and humanity, like our own—added to the enemy's relentless pursuit of our demise—have left us all in the roles of victims and victimizers.

Regardless of motivations, lies bring blistering results. The embers of dishonesty ignite and spread quickly, like wildfire, consuming human dignity. The person who lies scorches his self-perception, and the individual who is lied about is left singed by accusations. Those of us who buy into lies and live accordingly do so with a smudged reality. Like trying to drive our car with a mud-splattered windshield, it's hard to see past the dirt. Deception is a game Satan takes delight in, hoping to plant in our hearts and minds falsehoods so that, in believing them, we unwittingly pass them on.

Nehemiah recognized the need to protect his people from the enemy's aggression and so provided his workers with weapons—weapons they valiantly held in one hand while diligently laboring with the other. The strategy proved successful, which gives us reason to consider carefully Nehemiah's tactics to help us combat our own dilemmas.

Weapon #1: Prayer

I believe the first tactic Nehemiah drew on to defeat the enemy was prayer. Scripture records Nehemiah's prayer as he turned his enemies over to God's judgment. "Hear, O our God, how we are despised! Return their reproach on their own heads and give them up for plunder in a land of captivity" (Neh. 4:4). How astute of Nehemiah not to allow the enemy to divert him from his task and to drain his energy with exhausting attempts to defend himself.

I, on the other hand, recently approached a woman with a list of legitimate reasons I couldn't attend a function. She looked at me quizzically and then asked, "Are you looking for absolution?" That statement jarred me into realizing that, once again, I was wearing myself out, not to mention everyone else, with my need to defend my decisions. A defensive spirit is taxing, whether it's birthed out of our insecurity, our need for people's approval, our guilt, or our reluctance to face truth. The Lord is helping me to see that, like Nehemiah, when I make a decision based on prayer, I need to rest in it.

A few months ago, my husband Les's growing physical disability forced us to think about moving out of our old-fashioned, two-story home. We priced renovating the house but found it would be costly and quite involved. So we decided to put it on the market and to buy a house more suited to our long-term needs. The "For Sale" sign was up only two days before we had accepted an offer.

Then second thoughts invaded my mind. Would I always regret leaving this house I loved? Would the new house ever feel like home? Should we just have paid the price for the renovation? As these doubts assailed me, I struggled to remember that Les and I had prayed for direction, received a response, and acted on it. Now was the time to rest in what had been revealed to us. Otherwise, the adversary's tactic would be to drain me to the dregs as I jumped through exhausting emotional hoops.

Weapon #2: Choosing to Work

In addition to praying and leaving the enemy's fate in God's hands, Scripture states, "the people had a mind to work" (Neh. 4:6). The builders of the wall had set their minds to do what needed to be done. The habit of establishing our thoughts brings focus. And focus protects not only our minds but also our hearts from the splintering effects of indecision.

At some point after joining the ranks of the midlifers, I started to find it easy to waver in my decision making. I noticed Les and I often would stay home and snack for a meal rather than face the dilemma of choosing at which restaurant to eat.

Apparently the energy it took to figure out a solution wasn't worth it to us. Then I began to hesitate on other choices as well, and while the world wasn't going to tilt on its axis because I couldn't make up my mind, I found it disconcerting to be so unsure of myself. So I've set out to practice being more deliberate.

But how many of us fret over gnats while others are slaying dragons? Several months ago, I read Gwen Verdon's obituary in the *LA Times*, and I was struck by the deliberate decisions she and her mother made early on in Gwen's life. As a very young child, Gwen developed rickets, which left her legs weakened. By the age of two little Gwen had to wear corrective boots and already was suffering from the insensitive name-calling of other children. Soon she was tagged "Gimpy."

Gwen's mom was a dancer and knew how the discipline of dance had built strong muscles for her; so she decided to enroll young Gwen in dance. I'm sure some people thought that choice unwise. They probably shook their heads and rolled their eyes as Gwen awkwardly toddled by, but that didn't stop Gwen and her mom.

By the age of six, Gwen had traded in her old name for a new one, "The world's fastest tapper." As an adult, she went on to win a Tony and danced her way through lead roles in *Can-Can*, *Sweet Charity*, *Chicago*, *Damn Yankees*, and many other Broadway hits. Critics agreed that "Gwen Verdon was to Broadway dance what Ethel Merman was to

71

Broadway song." On the day of her death, at 8:00 P.M., the lights of Broadway were dimmed in her memory. All this from a little girl nicknamed Gimpy who chose to have "a mind to work."[1]

And to think I can't decide which restaurant to eat at. Oh, brother. I'm sure both Gwen's and her mom's hearts were broken many times as they worked to overcome her deficit. And I'm sure self-pity knocked on their door. ("Poor Gwen, not like other children.") Dance routines are difficult if both legs are strong; yet the Verdons made a decision, and Gwen tapped her weak little legs right onto the Broadway stage.

Gwen—and Nehemiah—probably realized something that's slowly dawning on me: Indecision leads to confusion, and confusion can lead to self-pity. Self-pity then leaves a toehold for the enemy, who loves to rouse our inner uncertainty, resulting in mental weakness. It's tough to have a "mind to work" in such a frazzled state; whereas mental decisiveness strengthens our ability to resist unhealthy temptations, resist the accuser's lies, and resist throwing highfalutin, royal pity parties.

Life is chock-full of unfairness, have you noticed that? When you mix unfairness with the enemy's lie that we're on our own, the result is a full-fledged, slathered-in-misery pity party . . . with monogrammed invitations, engraved "me, me, me." Usually few show up for this kind of shindig unless they arrive with a big box of their own unhappiness to unwrap in the presence of company.

Today, as I write, is Thanksgiving. Our home was

to be bustling with family, including our only grand-child, while aromas of turkey, biscuits, and yams permeated the rooms. But alas, our home smells more like an infirmary. Vicks assaults my nostrils while puffs of steam from the vaporizer cause my hair to hang limp. My dear husband came down with a whopping case of the flu with fever, chills, and a hacking cough so we had to cancel our company. Now, while I press computer keys in between delivering him his meds, he lies shaking under a mound of blankets in his pajamas.

In the past, the temptation would have been to see the melodrama (sniff, sniff) in our holiday quandary. Oh, woe is me! This kind of "why me" left me an easy target for the enemy's lies of how disappointing my life was. Instead, on this quiet holiday, as I sit alone, I remain very aware of and deeply grateful for the full life the Lord has allowed our family to share. And that, for me, friends, is measurable progress.

When Jerusalem's enemies heard of the progress the Jews had made on the building of the wall, the enemies announced their intentions both to stop the work and to kill the people. (Talk about cranky!) Nehemiah, alerted to the danger, immediately added to his arsenal of prayer and kept the builders focused on their goal. He then handed out weapons: shields, swords, bows, spears, and breastplates (Neh. 4:16). In addition, he positioned men in the lowest parts of the wall, the exposed places, and he stationed the people in families (Neh. 4:13).

I have, during low times, fallen prey to the fiery

darts of the accuser. Our enemy celebrates our down times and cattily awaits a chance to pounce on our vulnerability with his lies. "If God loved you—really loved you—he wouldn't allow you to suffer this way. He says he will never give you more than you can bear, but look at you, why, you're down and out." He wails and whines on and on, pressing against tender emotions and deep-seated fears. Obviously, we, too, need additional weapons distributed to us if we are to combat Satan's treachery and walk in Christ's victory.

Weapon #3: The Shield

The sword and the shield, used to protect Nehemiah's people, helped to ward off attacks and hold on to territory. I was fascinated to learn that many shields used in biblical times were made of a wood imbued with a natural quality that extinguished flames, which is certainly helpful when the enemy is hurling fiery arrows. "In addition to all, taking up the shield of faith with which you will be able to extinguish all the flaming missiles of the evil one" (Eph. 6:16).

Also, shields were bowed and carved out in back so that one could crouch down inside and find refuge out of the line of fire. The psalmist David put it this way: "He [God] is a shield to all who take refuge in Him" (Ps. 18:30b).

How does God become our shield? When we make up our minds to trust him. Hmm, we're back to a mind-set. Powerful weapon, the mind. You see, prior to Nehemiah's arrival, the people were scattered and scared, but once he came on the scene and told them how God had provided for them through the Persian king, they had a strategic shift in their thinking. Their circumstances hadn't changed, but their reasoning had. They positioned their minds to trust God anew and relinquished their rights to always understand his ways in this broken world.

When my only brother, Don, was killed in a car accident, I was afraid I'd lose my faith in God. I hurt so deeply, and I couldn't make sense of Don's death, especially since he left behind a wife and six children who needed him. I thought if his death made sense, somehow we could live with it. Yet, through the loss and grief, my faith gradually grew stronger as I took refuge in the Lord, running to him with my anger, my doubts, my fears, my pain, and especially the future.

A great many things God does or doesn't do are a mystery. I often don't get it. When I acknowledge that my mind is finite and when I enter into his will, even reluctantly, then all that puzzles and perplexes me falls under the mysterious facet of God's character. In so doing, I acknowledge my limited thinking and acquiesce to his fathomless ways. This is, for me, comforting and liberating, as I remind myself that I'm not in charge (rats!) and that our gracious, merciful God has plans far beyond my narrow thoughts (whew).

When I don't take refuge in the Lord, sheltered behind the shield, the enemy reaches for arrows of doubt, suspicion, and uncertainty that he aims at my broken heart.

Weapon #4: The Sword

The sword represents the Word of God in our weaponry and is crucial to our triumph. Scripture offers us foundational fortitude, a place to stand sure-footed in this wobbly global community that we reside in, a world whose values seem to change with every new political agenda. Lord, help us! And he does, as the Word counsels us deeply, corrects us profoundly, protects us vigorously, directs us daily, and is the only offensive weapon listed in the spiritual arsenal God presents to us in the Book of Ephesians. The Word is also the best siren available to detect lies and to stave off the evil one when we're in low places (valley times) or exposed places (vulnerable moments).

We see Nehemiah's passion and honor for the Word when it is read to all the people by the prophet Ezra. Nehemiah announced that the reading of the Word makes that day a holy day. The people wept at the reading but Nehemiah told them, "Do not be grieved, for the joy of the LORD is your strength" (Neh. 8:9–10). He knew that the truth of the Word would dry their tears, deepen their joy, and equip them for every battle.

Weapon #5: The Breastplate

The breastplate is critical during battles, for it protects vital organs. The weight and awkwardness of the ancient breastplate meant the warrior required assistance to suit up. The breastplate is associated in the Bible with righteousness, which I must say is a weighty subject and an awkward fit for humanity. Christ, who is our righteousness, assisted us as he filled God's rigorous requirements on our behalf. As we choose to wear the breastplate (act rightly), with his empowerment, we help to safeguard our hearts from the assaults of this world.

Nehemiah responded in a righteous way when he discerned a plot to defame him. A supposed friend told Nehemiah that, to protect himself from murder, he should flee to the temple to hide. Nehemiah, understanding that only priests should ever enter God's temple, replied, "Could one such as I go into the temple to save his life? I will not go in" (Neh. 6:11). As soon as he took this stand, he realized he was talking to a betrayer who intended to bring Nehemiah down. Using the breastplate of righteousness, Nehemiah not only acted rightly but also ultimately saved himself from his enemies' plot.

Weapon #6: The Family

When Nehemiah positioned his people for warfare, he stationed folks in families. I'm sure it strengthened the people to be shoulder-to-shoulder with their loved ones, as they made a difference together while they protected each other's welfare.

We live in a society where families, like autumn

leaves, are scattered throughout the land, making connectedness difficult. But miles can't separate hearts nor, in our mobile society, can they keep us from one another's side during tough times.

One of my favorite families who exemplified shoulder-to-shoulder combat through difficult life-seasons was the March family of *Little Women* fame. Mrs. March and her four daughters faced financial reversal, the loss of husband and father while he was away at war, meager food supplies, and severe illness (of the youngest daughter).

While they are a fictional family, they serve as an example of how real families were designed to function. The Marches committed themselves to each other and also extended a helping hand to the needy. They worked at supporting one another, and together they made it through the financial and food short-ages, Mr. March being wounded, and their sister's death. The mother and father set an example, and the girls followed in their footsteps. (So, too, when our family members follow in our footsteps, may those tracks lead them to Jesus.)

What a fine reminder the Marches are of how important our families can be to our well-being, espe-cially during threatening times. I say "can be" because not all families are prepared or equipped to help us through attacks, or they may even be the ones attacking, which is probably why the Lord extended our first families with the family of God. He knew we would need a backup plan.

Now, let's survey our arsenal by listing some of the

ways to combat the enemy's lies, threats, and attacks: prayer, making up our minds, taking refuge behind our shield, carrying our sword (reading and knowing Scripture), wearing our breastplates (acting rightly, empowered by Christ), and lining up with our families. What a divine plan.

The world may be broken (and those of us in it), the enemy may be cunning (his termination is near), but we have options—divine options—that give us more than a fighting chance. All we have to do is remember we're in a battle and act accordingly. The enemy likes nothing better than for us to be oblivious to his tactics, agendas, and campaign so he can easily scatter our life-efforts and further break our hearts. Battles await us, but we have the equipment to stand fast and defend ourselves. So suit up, soldiers, we have work to do!

Lord Commander, help us shoulder our responsibility and remind us to take refuge in your righteousness. You, and you alone, are our help in times of trouble. Thank you that in you we are victors.

HEART MENDERS

Is there a weapon listed above that you aren't using? Why? Do you have trouble being decisive? How can making up your mind strengthen you? What lie(s) are you aware of that the enemy uses against you? How are you combating his attacks? Who is winning?

NEXT
_____

Armor in place, we now need to roll up the sleeves of our faith as we, in the next chapter, begin the work of growing stronger by building more wisely.

CHAPTER EIGHT

A Mighty Fortress: Everybody Needs Walls

TO DO.

Read Nehemiah 2:11–15.

Usually I don't care for walls. I'm more a sociable fence kind of person. I like to tip my hat, have a friendly chat, and then carry on with my day. Of course, I've been fortunate through the years that my neighbors have been, uh, neighborly. No howling dogs at midnight, no raucous party throwers, and no hooligans—nary a one. Oh, okay, maybe one. Yet I've never needed a keep-out-the-neighbor wall.

(Wait—one time I was sorely tempted to back in a cement truck and pour a wall. A rotund, middle-aged neighbor took up parading around his yard in a Speedo. Not a pretty sight. But then he moved. Whew!)

Walls actually are famous for far more than blocking an unpleasant view. For instance, the Berlin Wall was erected August 13, 1961, in the night while Berliners slept. It stood for twenty-eight years, dividing the city. Watchdogs, watchtowers, bunkers, and a second wall deterred people from scaling the wall. Many lost their lives trying to escape all the hostility and division it symbolized before it was torn down.

The Great Wall of China curves across the land like a sleeping dragon. Nearly three thousand miles long, it required millions of workers to construct. It was built to guard the Chinese northern border, and now is a national treasure representing generations of effort and ancestral pride.

The Wailing Wall in Jerusalem comprises the holiest of Jewish sites where people take their heart-cries to Jehovah. The Wailing Wall represents a nation's ongoing needs.

Jerusalem had a need during Nehemiah's time, and his heart-cry was for his people's safety. They had territorial issues with their surrounding neighbors, neighbors who presented a constant threat. So building the wall around the city was an issue of both wisdom and necessity. The wall sent a message to troublemakers that this city was a strong fortress and not one to be messed with. It also indicated that not everyone would find entry; individuals would need to be scrutinized first. And to the city's citizens, the wall signified safety and shelter.

Even though walls didn't prevent enemy attacks, they usually slowed or stopped the adversary's entrance—that is, unless the guards were dawdling at the donut shop. In that case, given the opportunity, rivals would overtake the city, plunder it, and then tear down the walls as a way to flex their superiority. Broken walls were a sign of the city's vulnerability and the enemy's ability to conquer.

When word reached Nehemiah that Jerusalem's walls were still down fifteen decades after the city had been devastated, he yearned to put things right. He knew the wall's condition meant his people were in a dire place and that the city limits were overrun with outsiders. Nehemiah's heart was stirred with holy concern as he journeyed to the ruins to survey the rubble.

In my mind's eye I imagine Nehemiah making his way through the damage, grieved by the desolation, while all the time designing a plan of restoration. That's so like Jesus. I'm comforted to realize that Jesus is moved by my pain and longs to redeem my losses. Heartache seems to arrive wrapped in loneliness and isolation that can cause us to feel forgotten and abandoned. Thank the Lord that he tearfully walks through our rubble while planning our sure future.

Heart Walls

If we think of Jerusalem as our hearts, then the walls become an important part of our defense against life's hardships. Walls of defense, as in Nehemiah's time, help us to ward off vandals (those who come to steal our joy), hooligans (those bent on stirring up strife), and rivals (those who are committed to derision and division). That image of protection causes me to better appreciate walls, for I need a place of refuge out of the blustery winds of circumstances.

Not that I'm a stranger to walls, especially ones we hide behind; I've actually built a few of those. Unfortunately, mine were constructed out of fear. As a former agoraphobic, I lost several years walling myself off by withdrawing from the mainstream of society. Instead of the walls protecting me, they imprisoned me, and like the Berlin Wall, my self-serving barriers needed to be pulled down.

I'm frequently asked how I recovered from such an emotionally debilitating disorder. My answers are never satisfactory to those seeking easy solutions, for I found my restoration sluggish at best. In fact, the first thing I had to do was what the people of Jerusalem did when they agreed to participate in the rebuilding—"made up their minds to work."

I grew up with parents who had a strong work ethic. My mom was a farm girl from a family of eight and was required to help with the endless chores. My dad was a town boy whose family of five struggled on a meager income, so he assisted by delivering cheese and pies and even digging ditches for the county. Yup, both my parents knew how to put their shoulders to the plow.

But I grew up during a time of plenty, and as a

teenager, I was required only to help clean house on Saturdays and to assist with my little sister. I resented and resisted both of those duties and escaped them at every opportunity.

So when, as a young married adult, I had to learn to be a worker, I found it a character-producing challenge. I felt embarrassed, as a wife and a mom, to have to learn to do what others had known about for years. I had to force myself to make the bed and to make it every day. What a drag. Of course, carrying around a five-hundred-pound backpack of depression didn't help to lighten my daily load. Quite honestly, I didn't think doing daily household duties was worth the effort. What possible benefit could it have anyway?

Yet as I made the bed, regardless of how I felt, along with doing the dishes, the laundry, and an assortment of other once-forsaken tasks, order began to form in my life. Not just physical order but also emotional and spiritual order. Along with order, a rhythm of personal respect began to develop, and I found I slowly was being released from the curse of my self-disgust.

Once my self-constructed defensive walls began to crumble, I then had to learn the benefit of God's walls of defense. Defensive walls, walls of defense—the two sound so close yet the difference is remarkable. Instead of my closing off others, I began to learn to open up to God. Instead of fearing life, I began to become fortified. And instead of being isolated, I began to learn spiritual vulnerability (a willingness to risk trusting God). And may I say, this was not fun! It was and continues to be hard work, like plowing a field or digging a ditch. The comforting part is, as I've heeded the Lord's counsel, I've grown, and today, at least most days, I even like myself.

Boundary Walls

Walls also demarcate boundaries. Some days do you feel as if you're on a battleground—even with those whom you love? I do. And sometimes I'm the one hurling grenades while loved ones take cover behind their walls. We sure don't want to brick off our families (well, there might be a few relatives), but we do need to mark our boundaries. Boundaries are those love-lines we establish that say, "I'm so sorry you're having a bad day, but you may not punish me for it." There's a big difference between support and indulgence, but sometimes that line is hard to distinguish. Separating ourselves from others' hostility keeps us from absorbing their anger, which has the potential of setting a match to our own (and we all have some).

Broken walls were a sign of Jerusalem's vulnerability (weakness) and are a sign of our own. For instance, a friend's betrayal, a child's rejection of a parent's values, or a coworker's harmful lies expose our unprotected hearts. For when we have had a skirmish with someone that has left us hurt and angry, it leaves a gaping, vulnerable place where resentment can reside. And resentment is one rowdy fellow who kicks dust in everyone's face. I'm sure that's why we're directed in Scripture not to "let the sun go down on [your] anger" (Eph. 4:26).

Recently a woman named Trudy wrote to me and confessed that for seventeen years she had resented her mother-in-law. During those years she restricted the mother-in-law's visits, all but cutting her off from her son and five grandchildren. Then tragedy struck; one of Trudy's children was the victim of a hit-and-run. Trudy was helpless and her heart shattered. During her grief, her mother-in-law came in and quietly loved her. Gradually Trudy's resentment toward her mother-in-law was replaced by regret, and the regret led to repentance before God and reconciliation between the two women.

Trudy closed her letter with these words: "If only I could give my mother-in-law back the years I stole from her, years of knowing our family, but we both thank God for the precious years left to us. How could I have known that she whom I found offensive would become my dearest friend?"

She signed the note, "Humbled by his grace, Trudy."

It is humbling when a wall of our making is demolished and suddenly we gain a new perspective.

In Italy the city of Lucca was fortified with walls that were built between the eleventh and thirteenth centuries because two dukedoms longed to incorporate Lucca into their holdings. Then, as artillery technology increased, Lucca had to replace this wall with a more substantial one, one that was higher and wider than any that existed before. So the people put their shoulder to the task and constructed a bruiser of a wall—forty feet high and ninety-eight feet wide at the base.

Then, after many decades, Lucca's citizens realized they were no longer under threat of invasion. Instead of tearing down the wall, the citizens decided to utilize it for themselves and their guests by making it into a promenade. Townsfolk and visitors today can still stroll around the wide, tree-festooned wall, enjoying the views of the city inside and the rolling land outside. Doesn't that sound hospitable?

One day—one forthcoming day—we won't require walls of any kind. We won't be under any threats of invasion, all artillery will be laid aside, all enemies dispersed, and instead we will promenade in high places with the most glorious views. "Eye has not seen and ear has not heard, . . . all that God has prepared for those who love Him" (1 Cor. 2:9).

Lord of High Places, thank you that you do not wall yourself off from us. Help us in return not to wall ourselves off from you. May we be wise in our construction and build according to your principles. And may you find us willing to disassemble any walls that are an offense to you. Teach us to promenade in your presence, enjoying the view.

HEART MENDERS

Do you feel battle-weary? Who are you battling against? How might you put this fight to rest? Where do you take refuge? While we need walls for refuge, other walls need to be dismantled . . . have any?

NEXT

A walled city without gates is nothing more than a prison. So grab your toolbox; we'll need to install places to enter and exit. And since it's a gate, we'll be entering, let's do so with a heart of thanksgiving (Ps. 100:4).

CHAPTER NINE

Silent Sentries: Gates to the Heart

TO DO.
_____

Read Nehemiah 6:1.

I love gates, especially well-tended ones. They suggest preparedness, privilege, and privacy. And gates give me a sense of adventure, especially when I swing open a gate and discover a path to follow. If you have a brick path that leads to a covered porch with a waiting cushioned rocker, honey, I'm your newest houseguest.

Gates that guide one into gardens are equally wonderful. Nothing is more heartening to my road-weary soul than to wind my way through petunias, peonies, and poppies, especially when the path opens from a gate. Gates add romance, especially to a floral setting.

Although in Japan, posted on the gates of one of their botanical gardens, is this sign: "No picnicking, no botanizing, and no uproaring in these gardens." Hello? How much fun is that?

Gates that once led us to people we loved are nostalgic as well. The sights and sounds are synonymous with the cherished visits we paid. The clanking sound as the latch popped open and the joyous groans as it was swung ajar nest in our memories and warm our hearts.

Much more than nostalgia caused Nehemiah and his people to prioritize the repairs on the city gates. For if intruders overtook the city's gate they had won the city. Well-built, well-guarded gates were critical to the citizens' security and also to their prosperity, for most business transactions took place at the gates. Important decisions were made, laws were established, court was held, and social interactions took place at the gates. Opening the gates was as important as closing them.

When I consider the significance of a gate to a city, I can't help but think about the gate that opens into our minds. Our minds have the capacity for reasoning, creativity, and foolishness. It's that last one that throws the monkey wrench into the mechanism. I've learned through the years that thoughts are powerful forces that can influence our health, our attitudes, and our relationships with others and with God. Therefore, we must tend to the gates within ourselves.

The Sheep Gate

During the rebuilding in Nehemiah's day, a number of entrances offered access to the city. Each of the gates had a main function that was represented by that gate's name. Scholars disagree as to how many gates existed and whether their names overlapped. We do know, for instance, sheep were bought and sold at the Sheep Gate. How grateful I am that we are the Lord's sheep, and no one can buy us, for we were purchased with his blood. (Not even thirty pieces of silver can change that.)

Our thoughts are our sheep, and we need to decide which ones we're going to claim and which ones we're going to let go. For example, did you know we can think ourselves sick? I once developed allergy symptoms to a bouquet of flowers and then later found out they were silk! Ah...ah...choo! How embarrassing. And more than once a night creak in the house grew in my mind from a mouse to a rat to a gang of thugs, when in fact it was a creak in the house. My hubby quipped, "The only thing worse than a creak in the night is a pain in the neck." Well!

Thoughts can even wake us up. More times than I can count I've gone to sleep knowing that I have to wake up at a certain time to catch an early flight and the following morning, one to two minutes before the alarm jingles, I awaken. That's amazing since normally I sleep like a sloth and could snooze through a bongo competition.

Thoughts can inspire us and help us to make important changes but, alas, they also can deceive us. The prince of the power of the air, Satan, uses the airwaves to deliver thoughts that can mislead, intimidate, confuse, entice, discourage, frighten, and corrupt. And he is committed to these tasks in hopes of deluding and dissuading us. Add to that our own human tendency toward selfishness, and obviously a well-hung gate on our minds is a must. Then we can choose to escort some thoughts in and usher others out.

We need to monitor which sheep we allow into our hearts, too. Have you ever confided in someone only to have him or her use the information against you? I have. It makes you want to weld the gate closed and take up sheepshearing. Yet the Lord asks us to be open, lest we miss receiving his blessings, which he often sends through the lives of (sheep-y) people.

I don't believe we can guard our hearts from all hurts, but I do think we can be wise about which sheep we allow into our inner circle. We do need God's counsel and the Holy Spirit's promptings because some really neat sheep can initially appear to be wolves, and vice versa. We tend to appraise others by outward appearances, while God sees to the core of a person's being.

When I first met Les I knew instantly he was not for me. When he showed interest in me (by pretending to run me over with his car), I thought, *How rude!* I told my friend, "Those other guys might be nice, but I sure don't like that driver!"

Les and I stepped through the gates of matrimony thirty-nine years ago, and may I say he can run over me any time he wants (figuratively). Had I gone with my first assessment, I never would have had the pleasure of knowing what a dear man, what a thoughtful husband, and what a devoted daddy Les is.

Not that we haven't had our share of struggles; in fact, many times we could have put the next gate to good use . . .

The Refuse Gate

The Refuse Gate, also known as the Dung Gate, was the city's sanitation system. It was the gate where the waste was taken out and disposed of south of the city in the Hinnom Valley. Not a pleasant thought but certainly a practical issue; otherwise the city would have teemed with disease.

For us the Refuse Gate represents an exit for the garbage in our lives. You know, those rotten thoughts we tuck deep in the recesses, those stale attitudes that keep us stuck, and those moldy ruminations that keep our hearts hostile and afraid. We have to remember to take advantage of our Refuse Gate and our Hinnom Valley.

Trash pickup in our neighborhood is on Thursdays. On Wednesday evenings you see folks up and down our street lugging their garbage receptacles out to the curbs. None of us want to miss having our garbage picked up because we know it would mean another week of stinky accumulation that would overflow into our garages and houses.

If we would be as vigilant with our heart trash, we would experience an internal freshening. That's what keeping short accounts with the Lord is all about. And get this: We don't even have to lug the stuff to the curb. Just drag it out into his presence, and he will take it from there. The Lord responds when we ask him to cleanse our thoughts, forgive our mischievousness, and free us from accumulated debris. Yes, the Refuse Gate is imperative so we do not live in dis-ease.

The Fountain Gate

The Fountain Gate offered a source of fresh water from the mouth of the Siloam tunnel. I can almost picture women with water jars balanced atop their heads as they chatted about the latest village news while passing each other at the gate. The arid climate there required constant trips to the fountain.

Les and I usually spend a couple of months in the California desert during the winter. When we arrive, we're almost immediately affected by the lack of moisture in the air. Within days I have nosebleeds, my lips shrivel (yes, shrivel), and my body screams for water. Cool, clear, clean water. I am forced to slurp up bottles of H_2O like breath mints in an attempt not to dry up and blow away.

The Fountain Gate offers us a flood of good news, for water symbolizes the refreshing Word of God.

When we open this gate, truth pours in, and wisdom and understanding rinse over our parched souls. What a relief to go from the brittleness of this old world's thinking to the cool hydration of our minds.

Read Nehemiah 8 and be comforted, for you will see God's people replenished as they meet in front of the Water Gate and the Word of God is read to them. I love verse 10 where the people are told, "Go, eat of the fat, drink of the sweet, and send portions to him who has nothing prepared; for this day is holy to our LORD. Do not be grieved, for the joy of the LORD is your strength."

Before I latch the gate on this chapter, I must tell you about two of the most memorable gates I've ever seen. They weren't standing regally before a European castle or beckoning one to promenade celebrated gardens in some fruitful paradise. Instead they grace the National Memorial in Oklahoma City. The bombing that shattered Americans' hearts now has at the site, in place of the devastation, a stirring memorial. Stone gates set between heaven and earth that invite the public in to remember those whose lives were altered forever.

I had the privilege of visiting the memorial with two women who were both survivors of the bombing. To hear the stories from their perspectives was poignant. One of the women had been making a left-hand turn at the traffic light next to the building when it exploded; the other was across the street in a church office when the earth shook, glass shattered, and dust and death filled the air. The young woman whose van was blown across the street suddenly became an ambulance driver transporting the injured in her vehicle to the hospital. The woman at church assisted as the sanctuary became a temporary morgue. Never could they have imagined how a moment could change them forever or how courageous they would need to be.

As we entered through the East Gate into the memorial, the silence was palpable. Suddenly you didn't want to speak, and if you did, it was in reverent whispers. As I took note of others who were touring I saw in their faces tears, sadness, and disbelief. I felt the same.

The reflecting pool that ran between the East and West Gates mirrored our awareness of how broken this world is and brought an added contemplation to the setting. Sitting in rows on an incline overlooking the pool were empty chairs symbolizing those who died in the explosion. People stood riveted as they viewed the larger chairs, which represented the adults who died. Others wept openly on seeing the tiny chairs that represented the dear little lambs who lost their lives that horrific day.

Engraved on one gate is the time of 9:01; on the other is 9:03. They frame the moment—9:02 A.M.— of destruction. When we walked out the West Gate, I saw this inscription: "May this memorial offer comfort, strength, peace, hope, and serenity." And it does.

How appropriate that across the street from the West Gate stands a large, white statue of Christ, his head bowed as he weeps. What I saw as I studied the statue was our Lord anguishing over the loss of life, grieving for the survivors, and lamenting over the degradation of humanity's heart.

Yes, our world is broken, and our hearts do need mending from the devastation life brings us. That's why we turn to the Lord, who ushers his sheep into his city where the walls are called "salvation" and the gates "praise" (Isa. 60:18). He promises us that his city, where we will dwell, will never close its gates, for it will be a place of eternal safety (Rev. 21:25).

> *On earth, Lord, we have no lasting city, but we long for the one that is to come. We listen at the gates, and our hearts leap for joy at the sound of your shepherding, eternal voice. Come, Lord Jesus, and reign in our hearts.*

HEART MENDERS

What kind of sheep are you? What fills your thought-life? Have you scrutinized whom you've let into your gate? Do you need to schedule a trash pickup? What needs to be tossed out? Are you thirsty? How can your thirst be satisfied?

NEXT

Ever wish you could see above your circumstances? Our next chapter deals with a towering mentality, a higher perspective. If heights bother you, you might want to bring your meds and a parachute.

CHAPTER TEN

High Places: Watchtowers

TO DO.

Read Nehemiah 10:30–39.

Rapunzel, Rapunzel, let down . . . oh, no, that was a different kind of tower. The towers we're speaking of don't imprison princesses; they protect them. They are the towers used to guard gates around a walled city. We've already discussed that the gates were exceedingly vulnerable in Nehemiah's day; therefore, towers were erected for guards that they might observe and protect the entry.

Have you ever been in a tower? Being only five feet tall, I'm not much on heights, so I have a narrow frame of reference for anything over, say, five-foot one. I once climbed up a vacant lifeguard tower that was all of seven feet tall, and it took a friend and a lot of prayer and coaxing to get me back down.

I had two brothers-in-law, Bob and Fred, who for years did steelwork that required them to walk across narrow beams many stories up. They strolled across those six- to twelve-inch iron beams two hundred feet in the air as casually as we walk down a sidewalk. Just writing about it makes me nauseous. I don't have a steady horizon to begin with, and not being grounded throws my equilibrium into a spin. Spin . . . agh! I don't want to talk about it. Suffice it to say, if you have a tower and it needs guarding, don't hire me.

Towering Standards

Actually, we all need towers in the form of standards. The raising up (did I say "up"?) of a standard is a safeguard for our lives. It means we know whom we believe and what we believe and that we filter our behavior through that grid. Standards add vigor to our faith, and they help to protect us from distracting winds of doctrines.

The word *standard* is defined as "a principle that is used as a basis for judgment." When we raise a godly standard, it elevates us (not as in "puff up" but as in "grow up"), gives us a higher perspective (beyond our finiteness), and guards us against becoming casualties of the enemy's deceptions.

Two types of building are going on in the Book of Nehemiah: the rebuilding of the walls and the city, and the rebuilding of the people. We see them raising godly standards to live by. They pledged to walk in God's law, not giving their daughters to other peoples in marriage; forgiving debts after seven years; not dealing in commerce on the Sabbath; tithing not only money but also a portion of their dough, their fruit, their wine, their oil, their cattle, etc. (Neh. 10:30–38). After making this pledge, the people proclaimed, "Thus we will not neglect the house of our God" (Neh. 10:39b). These standards were not established to place a hardship on the people but to provide guidance for right living.

When I was twenty years old, I struggled to figure out how to "live right." I certainly realized that the way I was living wasn't working. I was flailing emotionally, physically, relationally, and spiritually. Out of my desperation, shortly after giving birth to my first son, I attended a tiny white church on a hilltop and gave my life to Christ. Soon after that experience, I found myself once again in a daily struggle for my sanity. My crisis peaked when I became so sick of myself that I was willing to risk making changes. (Which is why we shouldn't always rescue people who are in the throes of a crisis, for it might be the very platform that God is using to help set them in a much better place.) The journey to the end of oneself is different for each of us, but one telltale sign that we've reached it is when we develop a willingness to embrace God's way and valiantly work toward raising his standards.

You see, as an agoraphobic, I was frightened of

everything. I was afraid of being ill, and yet I constantly made poor choices regarding my diet and schedule. I was afraid of taking medication; yet I'd plead with my doctors to help me. I was scared of riding in cars and yet grumbled that I was isolated. I was in a no-win struggle, sabotaging my own recovery.

Then I began to memorize Scriptures on fear and courage, that I might change the way I thought and behaved. I would quote, "Casting down imaginations, . . . and bringing into captivity every thought to the obedience of Christ" (2 Cor. 10:5 KJV). I would say this over and over in an attempt to dislodge my faulty thinking and begin to raise a godly standard. It helped to convince my quavering heart that God had a plan of wholeness for me.

Another verse that fortified me was, "I can do all things through Him [Christ] who strengthens me" (Phil. 4:13). I especially appreciated that the apostle Paul had written that verse from prison since I was housebound and longed to have the courage to break free from my bars of fear.

"And the peace of God, which surpasses all comprehension, shall guard your hearts and your minds in Christ Jesus" (Phil. 4:7). His peace will guard my heart and—I love this part—my mind. Imagine the peace of God standing in our tower guarding our gate. That image helped to comfort my fractured, frightened mind.

Finding Fellow Changers

During this change-point in my life, I took a big step in learning how to raise a standard when I began to attend a small Bible study with other women who wrestled with their inadequacies. They, too, were broken and in the process of mending. They were farther along than I was emotionally and spiritually, and it helped me to observe their victories and new behavior. Then I would go home and practice living out truth. Sometimes it went quite well, but other days I felt like I was doing the cha-cha—two steps forward, one step back. I think that's how we learn any new rhythm—advance, advance, step back, step back, advance, advance, step back, step back— whether it's a dance routine or life's cha-cha- changes.

Sometimes we find ourselves in a place where we don't have the encouragement of others to teach us new dance steps. Where do we turn at that point? Nehemiah was in a lonely place of leadership when he moved to Jerusalem to work on the wall. We find him recording in his journal times of aloneness. "I consulted with myself" (Neh. 5:7a); "I did not tell anyone what my God was putting into my mind to do for Jerusalem" (Neh. 2:12); "I went up at night by the ravine and inspected the wall. Then I entered the Valley Gate again and returned. And the officials did not know where I had gone or what I had done" (Neh. 2:15, 16a). In some seasons of our lives, we are called to stand alone, which gives us the opportunity to deepen our friendship with God.

Beyond Babbling

Another standard I needed to raise was that of my speech. I talked too much, and I promise you, nobody—absolutely nobody—wants to hear the *Encyclopaedia Britannica* spouted to him or her in one sitting. I needed severe editing and should have followed the advice of a plaque I once read: "Dear Lord, please put your arm around my shoulders and your hand over my mouth." Unfortunately, I would have been competition for the Tower of Babel. So I began a word study on the mouth. Don't do that if you don't plan on changing—it's way too convicting.

Even though on occasion I'm still given to spurts of words, generally speaking, my friends find me to be quite quiet. Now that, folks, is proof that raising a standard is worth the effort—and also that miracles still occur.

Some of the verses that particularly stood out and became part of my mental guidelines were, "A gentle answer turns away wrath, but a harsh word stirs up anger" (Prov. 15:1). My retorts tended to light fires, but this new standard of a soft answer helped to quell the ignition on both sides. "A word fitly spoken is like apples of gold in pictures of silver" (Prov. 25:11 KJV). This Scripture stirred my heart, as I was reminded of the value and beauty of a well-placed word.

I noted Nehemiah's vocabulary as he instructed

the people and bolstered their spirits as they labored on the wall. To persuade the people that they were capable of accomplishing that which hadn't been done in 150 years—erecting the wall—he simply said,

> "You see the bad situation we are in, that Jerusalem is desolate and its gates burned by fire. Come, let us rebuild the wall of Jerusalem that we may no longer be a reproach." I told them how the hand of my God had been favorable to me, and also about the king's words which he had spoken to me. Then they said, "Let us arise and build." (Neh. 2:17–18)

Obviously, by the influence he had on others, this was a man who selected his words wisely and well. We see him persuasively placing his words before the king regarding Nehemiah's and Jerusalem's futures (Neh. 2:2–6). We hear him convincing rich people to give back to the poor that which shouldn't have been taken in the first place (Neh. 5:6–12). Yes, Nehemiah drew carefully from his well of words, refreshing his hearers and replenishing their courage.

This next verse helped me to realize that both my mouth and my heart needed to be scrutinized by the Lord. "Let the words of my mouth and the meditation of my heart be acceptable in Thy sight, O LORD, my rock and my Redeemer" (Ps. 19:14). Sir Walter Scott reminds us that such scrutiny is important not only for our sake but also for those in the vicinity of our words when he says, "Many a word, at random spoken, may soothe or wound a heart that's broken."

I had so many hurdles to jump in my development that I felt like an Olympic runner. Little did I realize that twenty-five years later I'd still be huffing and puffing on the track. I thought it would be a short sprint, and then I could bronze my track shoes. Instead, at this juncture of the marathon, the types of hurdles have changed, but they are still there. And I've learned that we weren't meant to step off the track until the race is finished. And honey, the race isn't over until the "fluffy" lady sings, "When the roll is called up (did I say 'up'?) yonder, I'll be there."

Left to our own devices, Lord, we tend to settle for less than your best. Help us to lift our sights to your standards. May our faith tower, allowing our vision to soar above our circumstances.

HEART MENDERS

What standards have you raised? What standard do you know you need to raise? How might you do that? What stands in your way?

NEXT

Ever wish you could hang a "Go Away" sign on your door? Our next chapter gives you permission to do exactly that. What's that I hear? Is someone knocking?

CHAPTER ELEVEN

Knock, Knock: Doors and When to Open Them

Read Nehemiah 7:1–3.

I'll never forget the day the operating room doors swung wide and my youngest son walked toward us, holding his newborn baby, our first grandson. Through that door, joy entered our lives.

I'll also never forget when I opened my front door and found a woman standing there with anger in her eyes and animosity in her heart. She had come to stir up strife between some church members and me. My lack of an educational degree was an affront to her, and she felt I shouldn't be teaching a Sunday school class. Through that door, discouragement and disenfranchisement entered my life.

Doors, when opened, can bring joyous or jolting messengers. Good news: We don't have to swing open the door to every knock. That's the benefit of door-knobs, peepholes, and dead-bolt locks. Whew!

Actually, you're probably wondering, if we already have walls, gates, and towers, why would we also need doors? Because you have to have more than good defenses; you have to have a good strategy. After all, Jerusalem had all the necessary defenses, but when the people let down their guard and left ajar their gates and doors, they were overtaken with calamity (Neh. 1:3).

I've been there. Not to Jerusalem, but overtaken. I've opened my door more than once, and there she stood, old Calamity herself. Sometimes Calamity came in the form of financial distress. Sometimes she was relational havoc or illness or a frenetic schedule or depression or all of the above. When Calamity rapped, I opened the door. She would skitter in past me and run slipshod through my life, causing mayhem.

I'm grateful to say that eventually another tapping would sound on my door (or jingle on my phone), and it would be Nehemiah—in the form of one of my friends—to help me repair the door, close it, and lock it again. That is, once we threw out Calamity.

One person who taps on our doors that we would want to respond to is Jesus. He often can be heard knocking, knocking at our hearts' doors. It's his way not to skitter in but to wait for our invitation. He also proclaims by the authority of the Father that he

(Jesus) *is* the Door, the Door through which we enter into acceptance and relationship with God.

Armored Door

In Nehemiah's time, doors were made of wood with sheets of metal; some were constructed of one slab of stone. They had bolts or locks and keys.

Doors, to me, often appear invincible. I'm drawn to double doors because they sport twice the hospitality and are doubly invitational. Arched doors always pique my curiosity, while screen doors that creak with history make me nostalgic. French doors charm, Dutch doors divide, carved doors impress, and glass doors reveal. Of course, most of the doors I've mentioned are more about aesthetics than armament. What we need are heavy-duty doors with solid hinges and a peephole so we can invite in the right folks and latch out Calamity and her friends. And that's the most important factor about doors—knowing when to open and when to close them.

I once was sleeping in a hotel in California when, about one in the morning, a man pounded on my door and yelled, "Fire!" Startled awake, I jumped from my bed and tried to make an assessment as I heard the man continue down the hall knocking on other doors. I didn't smell smoke so I ran to the window and looked outside where I saw neither smoke nor fire trucks. I listened for a moment and heard no sirens. I ran to the door and felt the wood. It was cool to the touch. I then called the front desk and was told they were unaware of any problem. After reporting the incident to the hotel security, I climbed back in bed and fell asleep. The next day I was grateful that, despite my excitable personality, I hadn't raced to the door and flung it open to who knows what or whom. Of course, with my flannel nightgown and my bed-head hairdo, I might have scared the fire out of him. There definitely is a time to keep the door firmly closed. How grateful I am for dead bolts, locks, and keys.

But sometimes we need to open our doors to help others. I've been the grateful recipient of more than one open door.

Some years ago Les and I, along with our young son, Marty, and our baby, Jason, left our friends' house after midnight and headed for home, a fifteen-mile drive. That winter's night our trusted car came to an abrupt halt on the side of the road. Temperatures were dangerously cold, with the windchill factor hovering around thirty-five degrees below zero. Les stepped from the vehicle to check under the hood, and immediately our windows frosted over. No homes were in the area, and the nearest help was several miles away. An occasional car passed by, with each of them making wide circles to avoid us. No one was willing to risk opening his door.

About the third time my eyebrows iced over, a vehicle that had passed us turned around and pulled up behind us. Then a second car pulled off the road in front of us. The car that returned was driven by a woman who said she saw Les staring down into the engine, and she knew the temperature was too cold to make repairs. The second car's driver was a man who carried a chain for towing. He offered to pull our lame duck to a service station. I climbed out of our car with the children, and we climbed into the woman's open doors so she could take us to a warm restaurant until Les picked us up. How grateful we were for two people who were willing to take a risk and open their doors to us.

How do we know when it's safe to open our door? We can't always tell by appearances how safe a person is. I mean, I've seen some good-looking serial killers on television, haven't you?

My former pastor and dear friend, Marv Valade, told me of a time he wished he hadn't opened a door. One early October morning, he went over to the church. The building was dark so Marv moved from one room to another turning on lights. But when he stepped into a hall, in the shadows loomed a figure in a frightening mask, and the figure was brandishing a hatchet. Marv said later he wanted to run, but only one foot was willing to go with him. His heart was hammering when the figure leaned over and began to guffaw. The monster lifted his mask to reveal one of Marv's playful parishioners—trick-or-treating, I guess. Marv still nervously chuckles about that memorable door-opening moment but has since secured his premises.

Nehemiah also understood the importance of having doors in place to bar out unwelcome "guests."

In his journal he recorded, "It was reported to San-ballat, Tobiah, to Gesham the Arab, and to the rest of our enemies that I had rebuilt the wall, and that no breach remained in it, although at that time I had not set up the doors in the gate" (Neh. 6:1).

In the next chapter, he noted that—whew!—the doors were now in place. "The wall was rebuilt and I had set up the doors" (Neh. 7:1). He then laid down guidelines for when the doors were to be bolted and unbolted, immediately putting into place a strategy for letting in the good guys but keeping out the bad ones (Neh. 7:3).

Who's There?

Probably all of us have entertained a few monsters in our lifetimes, which could convince us to hot-glue the door shut and not risk any pranksters. Yet Scripture reminds us, "Do not forget to entertain strangers, for by so doing some people have entertained angels without knowing it" (Heb. 13:2 NIV). I sure wouldn't want to miss an angel.

I've heard angels ascend and descend, but did you know they are bilingual?

My friends Ginny and Alan Lukei discovered that when they visited Italy. One day they decided to take a train to several small towns and look around. In their rush to catch the train they forgot to write down the name of the town where they parked their car. After a day of playing tourist, they began their journey back to the hotel where they had left their car, but none of the towns' names sounded right.

Alan and Ginny disembarked at one town, only to look around and realize nothing was familiar to them. The station was empty and dark, and they waited uneasily for an hour before another train came along.

They boarded that train and took it to the next stop. Again nothing looked as they remembered it. Several people were in the station at this stop, but none spoke English. The Lukeis fidgeted for another hour and boarded yet another train to the next town.

Much to their dismay, when they stepped onto the railway platform, they realized this wasn't right, either. Now they were a little frantic. Another hour ticked by, another train took them to yet another town, only for them to realize what they feared—they were hopelessly lost. It was eleven o'clock at night, they were in an unfamiliar country, didn't speak the language, couldn't find anyone to help them, and didn't even know what town they had left their car in.

Then Ginny noticed a lone woman sitting in a waiting area on the platform. Ginny approached her and inquired anxiously, "Do you speak English?"

"Why, yes I do," she responded sweetly.

Tears flooded Ginny's eyes as she dropped down in the seat beside the woman and poured out their story. The young woman reached in her purse and pulled out a cell phone. After learning the hotel's name where they had parked their car, the woman made calls to several towns until she found the correct one. She even had the hotel management go outside and verify the location of their vehicle. Soon the Lukeis were on one more train ride, but this one took them to the right destination, thanks to the English-speaking, cell-phone-carrying angel at the station.

Heaven Sent

I think the people of Jerusalem also must have seen Nehemiah as their heavenly messenger. He certainly spoke their language, answered their questions, and helped to get them on track. Nehemiah stepped through the door of obedience that his people might become wiser regarding the opening and closing of doors in their lives. We could take a few lessons.

First, install a peephole in the door of your life. Don't fling open the door before you know who is knocking. Sometimes you know you don't want to open the door just by taking the time to look.

Second, ask for identification. Once I invited in a man I thought was a repairman. Instead, I discovered he was a cult missionary. A goat will herd with sheep given the opportunity.

Third, enjoy visitors. Enter into nurturing, reciprocal relationships. They will bring gladness to you.

Fourth, establish a closing time. Even with the best of friends who have the best of intentions, we need to establish a time to lock up and be alone.

Those of us who have hearts in need of mending must establish patterns of not just opening our door because someone knocks. Not everyone should be allowed in—just ask the citizens of Jerusalem, my pastor, or me. But we should also be aware that sometimes the tapping at our door is a Nehemiah or an angel, come to throw out Calamity—just ask Ginny and Alan.

> *Gentle Savior, please come in and make yourself at home. We want our lives to reflect our relationship with you. Give us the discernment to know when to open and to close doors. And, Lord, when we entertain an angel, would you please ring the bells of heaven? We wouldn't want to miss it.*

HEART MENDERS

When did Jesus first knock on the door of your heart? Have you ever entertained an angel? What made you think so? Does your door have a peephole? What keeps you from using it?

NEXT

On the dusty road of life nothing is more appreciated than a cup of cool water. Our next chapter does even more; it guides us to the well. Oh, yes, if you want, feel free to bring your camels.

CHAPTER TWELVE

Well, Well, Well: Where to Go When You're Thirsty

TO DO.

Read Nehemiah 5:19; 6:9; 7:5a.

Without a fresh source of water, we're dust bunnies without a future. We're told to drink eight glasses of the wet stuff a day to maintain a healthy balance in our systems. I'm not much of a drinker; I'm more a chocolate-chip popper. But I must admit that, when I'm thirsty, nothing satisfies like a tall, icy tumbler of water.

Recently I was told that, when we sense we're thirsty, our bodies already have begun to dehydrate. If so, then thirst is our body's warning buzzer, and all we have to do is drink deeply to replenish our losses.

Now, here's my question: Do you think we have buzzers that go off to warn us when we are spiritually dehydrated? When our hearts are heavy from a dry season? I have a feeling, when we're a tad arid, others might notice our condition before we do. Hindsight tells me that my edgy responses, snippy attitude, and dim view of the future signal I need a trip to the well—the well of the Lord's presence, the well of his Word.

I wonder if we could devise a polite way to let each other know when we notice someone needs to visit the well. Perhaps we should have a pact with a trusted friend that, when we're spiteful, cantankerous, or moody, that person casually whispers, "Well, well, well." You might want to pick a friend with the gift of mercy. (It's very hard to deck a merciful person.)

I don't know if Nehemiah had a "well" friend, but he was an individual who understood the heart benefits of spending time in Jehovah's presence. His prayer life is evident throughout his journals; from the first chapter of the Book of Nehemiah until the last verse he consistently beseeched the Lord. Another indicator that he was spiritually attuned was his single-minded approach to the task at hand. He wasn't distracted, detained, or discouraged but stayed his course. Also, his ability to deal wisely with those who criticized him speaks of someone who drank long and deep at the well of wisdom. And Nehemiah unswervingly loved God's people, which is a hallmark of a well-watered spiritual life.

I love some of God's people . . . usually. But all of them unswervingly? I don't think so. I know, I know, "Well, well, well."

Speaking of Wells . . .

In Middle Eastern countries like Israel, the water supply determined a town's location. In fact, many towns' names have a root word (*ayin* in Arabic and *beer* in Hebrew) for "well" in them. For example, Beer (Num. 21:16), Beer-elim (Isa. 15:8), Ain (Num. 34:11), and Enaim (Gen. 38:14). Several American towns reflect that same recognition of the importance of water: Edgewater, Watertown, Cedar Falls, Boyes Springs.

Of course, people didn't have running tap water in their tents or homes in Israel. Instead they used community wells. So it's not surprising that in Bible times wells were meeting places for people, whether they were watering their herds, carrying personal water supplies back for their families, or looking for a mate. Huh? A mate? Or so it would seem...

On Abraham's deathbed he made his most faithful servant swear that he would return to Abraham's homeland to find a wife for his son Isaac. The servant did as he promised and journeyed to Mesopotamia, to the city of Nahor. And where do you think he went to shop for Isaac's wife? Well, well, well.

He arrived at the well in the evening, when the women would come out to draw water. The servant prayed and asked the Lord to show him which woman should be Isaac's wife based on how she responded when he asked for a drink. "May it be that when I say to a girl, 'Please let down your jar that I may have a drink,' and she says, 'Drink, and I'll water your camels too'—let her be the one you have chosen for your servant Isaac" (Gen. 24:14 NIV).

No sooner did he have that conversation with the Lord than Rebekah, a beautiful, young virgin, filled her water jar. The servant approached her, and sure enough, Rebekah lowered her jar that he might drink and then offered to water his ten camels.

Now, folks, watering camels is no easy job. Those long-legged sand castles can slurp a desert dry, and those humps are like endless reservoirs. And if you, like me, think downing eight glasses of water a day is agony, be inspired by a camel that can guzzle gallons at a gulp. Rebekah was just one young woman with one jar, but she unhesitatingly went about the arduous task. When the servant heard her words and saw her willing heart, he fell on his face and worshiped the Lord for answering his prayers and the prayers of his master.

The signs of well-spent time in Rebekah's life are clear as we observe her eagerness to share what she had; serve a servant; and take on strenuous, unscheduled tasks with a hospitable heart. Yes, I think a spiritually watered life is obvious, especially in the details of a day. For often the daily responses show the nitty-gritty of our interior lives. Our stick-to-it attitude, our values, and the depth of our faith all display themselves.

Personally, I'm impressed with Rebekah's reactions to the twins Interruption and Inconvenience. I find that pair maddening when I'm on a personal mission, and invariably the duo shows up in telephone calls, unscheduled visitors, and unexpected demands.

I wonder how many times, when my heart has resisted disruptions and I've been unavailable to a stranger, I have missed a servant bearing news from the Master.

Refreshment for the Parched

I'm comforted when I read in the Psalms, "He [God] changes a wilderness into a pool of water, and a dry land into springs of water" (107:35). This says to me that, no matter how depleted my heart may be, the Lord can cause it to blossom again. And whether I am in a self-imposed barrenness because of my busyness and neglect, or a hard, dry season of affliction, he can bring life-giving moisture to my parched heart.

Another Rebecca has deeply touched my life. She is my eighty-five-year-old mom, who lives in Florida with my sister, Elizabeth, and her family. Mom has Alzheimer's, a desert affliction if there ever was one. She no longer knows her family. Only a few names are left in her parched vocabulary: Elvira and Pearl, two of her sisters who have both died, and also the name of Jesus. The latter she converses with regularly and often speaks of going home to be with him. We as her family are grateful that she continues to find her way to the well.

Several months ago a young woman, Julie Cochrane, wrote me a letter after hearing me mention that my mom had Alzheimer's and Parkinson's. She shared that her dad also had been through the throes of these long good-bye diseases. Her father, Vernon Hinton, was a talented man (musician, engineer, athlete) who was loved and respected. His family was saddened as they watched their beloved family member become more and more befuddled.

Julie told me that one day her mom entered the room where her dad was standing looking confused. "Is something wrong?" his wife asked tenderly.

Vernon's answer is forever written on their hearts. "I don't know who I am, but I know Jesus loves me."

I don't know what kind of desert you may be in, but Vernon's family and I pray that you know and are comforted by this wellspring of truth: Jesus loves you.

The springs of God's love were evident in the ways Nehemiah gave his life away for his people. His words of counsel and comfort were like water to the arid souls of the people. And his unending supply of wisdom was an obvious sign of his own thirst being quenched by his visits to God's well.

Oh, Wellspring of our Souls, may you find us, like Nehemiah, at the well drinking in your life-giving goodness. And may we have a Rebecca attitude as we enter into a day, that we might make room for others and especially room for you in our hearts.

HEART MENDERS

To whom have you been looking to find out who you are? What well are you drinking from? And why? What do you need to do to make your way consistently to the Lord's well?

NEXT

You might want to fill a canteen; the shadowlands are just ahead.

CHAPTER THIRTEEN

Shadowland:
When the Way Is Dark

TO DO.

Read Nehemiah 3:22.

The word *valley* is defined as "an elongated depression between uplands, hills, or mountains, especially one following the course of a stream. Also a place, period, or situation filled with fear, gloom, or the like."

I've visited both of those valleys; how about you? Actually, I lived at that second address for extended lengths of time.

I remember one very long year when my schedule was greater than my physical and emotional stamina. My last trip of the grueling speaking season was to Canada in November. I prayed the Lord would give me the strength to take the next step. Well, I made it through the engagement, but by the time I headed home I was way past exhausted; I was numb.

When I stepped off the plane, I tumbled down, down, down into the valley of burnout. Talk about an elongated depression; I thought I would never find my way out. The numbness did begin to lift after a couple of restful months, but the struggle was inch-by-inch before a sense of stability returned.

The valley views are so restrictive, which is why we think we'll never find our way out, but the lessons are plentiful and tend to go deep into our souls. That's the thing about valleys: They usually are fertile with truth. I've found that most of us initially respond to valleys the same way. We say to ourselves, "If I ever get out of here, I'll never come back to this place again." And even though we may end up paying a return visit, each time we do we learn more . . . more about who we are, what we are made of, and how we relate to others. Of course, what we do with what we learn often determines the value of our own counsel.

In the Book of Nehemiah a valley verse caught my eye. Actually, it was a phrase: "the priests, the men of the valley, carried out repairs" (Neh. 3:22). I wondered if folks in that day referred to them as "the men of the valley." They were priests, God's called men, and they found themselves in a low place. And surely it was a down time since their city was in ruins, their people scattered, and they had been relegated to valley living.

It doesn't seem to matter if we are priest or pagan,

rich or poor, male or female, young or old, valley times come to us all. And I think sometimes we who treasure our faith are jolted because we think somehow our beliefs will deflect hard times. In truth, many of God's people have lived some of their most vital years, making their greatest contributions to others, while in deep valleys. Priests and peasants included.

Our broken hearts are especially consoled when someone volunteers to go into the valley with us. "The essence of giving comfort . . . is never to abandon the other person—to keep showing up, no matter what," Katherine Weissman, a hospice volunteer noted.[1] Nehemiah chose to enter the valley with his people when he made policy changes in how Jerusalem's governor should live. Former governors had laid burdens on the people, taking bread, wine, and silver from them. But when Nehemiah accepted that post, he wrote in his journal, "Yet for all this I did not demand the governor's food allowance, because the servitude was heavy on this people" (Neh. 5:18b). For twelve years he denied himself the governor's food allowance, sending a message of solidarity to those in the valley.

The Deeper the Valley . . .

For fifty-five years valley-trudger Amy Carmichael rescued children from the Hindu practice of temple prostitution. She fed, educated, and cared for defenseless children in India. Then, in 1931, she suffered a serious fall that left her crippled and later bedridden, but she persisted in her fight for the children and wrote books (*Candles in the Dark, If, Mountain Breezes*, etc.) that continue to touch heartstrings around the world.

The other night on television I watched *The Hiding Place*, the story of Corrie ten Boom, a Dutch woman who, with her family, was arrested for hiding Jews during Hitler's rampage. I hadn't seen the film in many years, and it reminded me of the atrocities of humankind and the difference faith makes. Corrie and her sister, Betsy, endured the same inhumane treatment in the concentration camps as the others; they were not spared because of their love for the Lord. But they believed that what was beyond their understanding God would sort out for good, and he owed them no explanations.

Corrie and Betsy lived in filth, with their bedding, clothes, and hair infested with lice. Yet they walked with clean hearts. They were severely mistreated, starved and manhandled. Yet they reciprocated with grace. The demands made on them were abysmal—stripped nude, taunted, and put through the rigors of hard labor. Yet they remained hopeful. Even though Betsy died while incarcerated, when Corrie was released from the hate camp she went on to minister to millions, a ministry hallmarked by love—a love forged more deeply in the valley of despair.

Corrie didn't come through her experience unscathed. Hardly. Her heart needed mending. She grappled with her beliefs and bitterness and had to decide in the midst of her nightmare what held true and who held her. Corrie had no choice but to walk through her valley, but she could choose to love her way through the valley and even beyond it.

Living in the Valley

When Christ's disciples joined him on a mountaintop, they wanted to build booths and remain there (Luke 9:33). Who wouldn't? The views were magnificent, and the company divine. But Jesus led them back down the mountain to the valley where they would walk out their faith. That's true for us, too. We may visit spiritual mountaintops, but more than likely, we will live out most of our existence in the lesson-laden valleys. The valleys of grueling work, disappointing people, financial reversals, devious enemies, untimely (from our perspective) deaths, and physical maladies, which seem to be part of our ongoing existence if not education on this dusty planet. No wonder folks sing with such gusto, "One bright morning . . . I'll fly away."

The Instruction Book

If I'm going to spend time in the valley, and I will, I want at least a hint—or better yet a handbook—to help me through. I like being informed. In fact, I appreciate the instructions flight attendants give regarding emergency procedures. Even though I've heard them a billion times and could sit up in the middle of the night and recite them backward, I'd much rather hear how to handle an emergency ahead of time than try to absorb the information while the plane is in a nosedive.

And I'm grateful that the Lord, likewise, has made emergency provision through his Word. The Bible is full of valleys and mountaintops and how folks survived and even thrived on their journeys. And this Handbook has survived the ages, that we might have hearts full of hope.

My dear friend Mary Graham shared about her deepest valley as we chatted the other day. She told me that her mom died at the age of seventy, which was a great loss for their large family. (Mary is the youngest of eight children.) When her mom passed, Mary's seventy-one-year-old father, inconsolable, took to his bed and died six weeks later.

Mary, stunned at the loss of both parents, found herself trudging through the valley of the shadow of death. Friends surrounded her and her siblings and brought with their caring spirits comfort.

But what went deep into the broken places to mend Mary's heart were the words from Psalm 23, "He restores my soul." She told me she had been familiar with those words all her life, but she didn't understand their meaning until she was in death's valley, as day-by-day, God did exactly that—he restored her soul.

Valley life is demanding, which is why I'm not surprised to find in the Book of Nehemiah our valley men, the priests, involved in the repair work. This tells me we had better roll up the sleeves of our faith and be ready and willing to enter even the valleys with a strong work ethic. As with Nehemiah's people, whether we are called on to mix the mortar, hang the door, or spit-polish the tower, let's go forth and do so with all our hearts, minds, and strength. For lowly work often leads to lifted spirits.

I heard an old song sung many years ago by a southern pastor and his wife, who at that time were in the valley of rejection. "I've got one more valley, one more hill, maybe one more trial, one more tear, one more curve in the road, maybe one more mile to go, I'll lay down my heavy load when I get home."

Remember, until you arrive home, valleys have rich soil from the mountain runoff; valleys are where the flowers flourish and the trees bear fruit. And valleys cause mountaintop views to be that much more breathtaking. So be cheered, for "He restores my [our] soul."

God of the Valley, may we not rush through the low places of our lives and miss the richness. The vista views are so restorative, but the roots deepen in the valley floor. Thank you for mountains, lest we forget to look up. And thank you for valleys . . . lest we forget to look up.

HEART MENDERS

Does your valley have a name? How long has it been since you enjoyed the vista from a mountaintop? Have you learned more from the mountain or from the valley? What words has the Lord spoken to your spirit?

NEXT

Give me a hand, would you? Oh, never mind, here comes Baruch. Don't you know him? Son of Zabbai. Well, come along, he's an exceptional fellow; I'll introduce you.

CHAPTER FOURTEEN

Worthy Hire: Help Wanted

TO DO.

Read Nehemiah 3:2; 8; 12.

The Book of Nehemiah is crammed with workers. That's good because, if you've ever worked on a church, school, or community project, you know how difficult it can be to find warm bodies. Besides, the only way the walls, gates, doors, towers, and homes could be repaired was if everyone was willing to do his or her part plus more. That meant from Grandpa down to Junior, from officials to gatekeepers, from merchants to priests, everyone needed to show up for roll call.

Quite honestly, I used to think genealogies (roll call) were boring until one day I traced one in Scripture and found the name of Jesus. That changed everything. Still, when I saw the list of workers in Nehemiah, I whispered to myself, "Do I care who did what?" And guess what? I do care because of what I learned.

I was heartened to see that people from every walk of life pitched in, stepping out of their comfort zones smack-dab into a military zone. They offered their time, skills, muscle, brains, and courage. Come along while I introduce you to just a few.

Seasoned Restorers

Meet "the men of Jericho" who came to build (Neh. 3:2). Now, what I wanted to know when their names were called out was whether their arrival was good news or bad. I mean, weren't the guys from Jericho the ones who, with a blast of some horns, brought the walls tumbling down? Listen, folks, if your walls fall because your neighbor is practicing his music lessons, you better talk to your mason; something's amiss with your mortar. But then I speculated, *These men should be seasoned, skilled wall-builders, since, once they took over Jericho, they had to go about the business of putting back up what they had just ripped down with their musical notes*. And a seasoned worker is to be prized.

Several years ago my friend Carol became seasoned in grief. She lost her adult son, Jeff, in a gun accident. During the months that followed his death, she learned that those who had gone before her, others who had experienced a child's death, extended the most understanding. Their words rang with clarity, their actions were well timed and full of tenderness, and their understanding of her emotions comforted profoundly. Like the experienced Jericho wall-builders, those who suffer loss have experience to offer fellow grievers. They have acquired mercy's touch that helps in the rebuilding of lives.

Sweet Smell of Volunteering

Two groups of people on the roll call who are unlikely candidates in my estimate for a rebuilding program are the goldsmiths and the perfumers. Their fields of expertise would have called more for eyeglasses and vials than gates and walls. Evidently that didn't keep them from venturing out and giving a hand.

Speaking of hands, theirs must have been tender initially, as the goldsmiths went from lifting molds to lifting boulders and the perfumers went from mixing fragrances to mixing mortar. What a change of pace!

I've found such changes are packed full of informational goodies. You see, every once in a while I have this wild idea that I would like to give up my speaking career and become a store owner. I think, *Wouldn't it be fun to drive a few miles to work instead of dragging my luggage through airport after airport? And wouldn't it be great to sleep in my own comfy bed instead of on a hotel log (well, it feels like one)? And eat at home instead of in repetitious restaurants with their Styrofoam dressing and where one is uncertain what is using your soup as a swimming pool? Wouldn't that be fun?* And yes, it was.

I have several friends who own stores, and they allow me to play store person any time I want. Of course, after a few weeks, I want to board a 747, check into a hotel, and order room service. Oh, don't get me wrong; I enjoy playing store, I love being home, and most of the time I can abide my own cooking. But I know my calling is to do what I'm doing. I promise you I wouldn't miss airports, but I'd miss people, and most of all I don't want to miss God's plan for my life.

Want to do something different from what you're doing now? Try it. It will either work or you'll return to your prior efforts with renewed zeal. Perhaps doing repairs was a good change of pace for the goldsmiths and perfumers, but I wouldn't be surprised if they were thrilled to return to purifying gold and crushing rose petals.

Noteworthy Workers

Among Nehemiah's workers, I enjoyed meeting Shallum. He was the son of Hallohesh, who happened to be the official of half the district of Jerusalem. Impressed? Shallum's daddy wasn't what drew my interest, though. It wasn't even who Shallum was, but instead it was what he did. He made repairs. I know, so did a lot of others, but it's what comes next that's noteworthy. He made repairs—with his daughters. Verse after verse lists the sons, but this is the only time the girls' team receives a mention. Yeah, girls!

Isn't Shallum's experience often true in life? Our reputations sometimes hinge on details that are a small part of who we are. As a matter of fact, sometimes what we've become known for is a far cry from who we are.

When I moved to a new house, I didn't know anything about my neighbor except that I had been warned she was a cranky lady. So, of course, I made wide circles around this gal to avoid any unnecessary conflict. But one day we met head-on with our snow shovels as we were clearing our adjoining sidewalks. Not able to ignore her, I offered a few token friendly words. She then did the same. The conversation went from insincere breeziness to a warm chatter that led in time to a delightful friendship. Like Shallum, the word on the street about my neighbor didn't really shed much light on who she was.

I'm sure my mom sometimes felt that way. Since I had a speaking and writing career, I was the better known of the two of us. So she often was introduced as "Patsy's mom." Well, one day I was introduced in her presence as "Rebecca's daughter." She was gleeful to think that, at last, she had been put in her proper place.

As in the cases of Shallum, my "cranky" neighbor, and my mom, it's easy to label others but hard to do so with precision. We're way too complex for that.

Fortunately, God is adept at seeing us every which way. Why, he's so into details, he oversaw the knitting of us together (puarl one, two, three) and right this minute knows how many hairs reside on our heads (and even if we've altered the color thereof). So much for reputations.

Standout Worker

Speaking of reputations, take a gander at Baruch. You know, son of Zabbai. You don't know? Well, let me tell you, out of all the people listed—priests, merchants, temple servants, and so on and so forth—Baruch is the only one to whom a certain characteristic is attributed. This characteristic evidently was so off the charts it needed to be recorded for future generations' benefit. The characteristic was one word, one lively declaration that caused me to star his verse. The word? *Zealously*. "Baruch the son of Zabbai zealously repaired another section" (Neh. 3:20).

Zealously—enthusiastically, keenly, passionately, eagerly, fervently, ardently, fanatically. Wow! Look at the energy portrayed in those synonyms. Makes me want to take a nap. Obviously naps weren't on Baruch's schedule; he was busy getting the job done, seeing it through to the finish, and doing so with zest. You go, Baruch!

I could sure use a big dose of Baruch, for I often sputter to a finish. Just check out my closets. No, please don't. I'd be embarrassed if you found the half-embroidered crib blanket I started more than a year ago for my first grandson, Justin. Justin is now six months old, and I was thinking my project might make a nice dorm blanket for when he heads to college, although the stitched carousel could cause a few stares. Or, in my closet, you might glimpse a black glittered holiday jacket with the tags still dangling. It's been hanging there three years waiting for me to hem the sleeves. And if you peek in, please pay no attention to the heelless boot or the broken purse strap; I plan to take them to the shoe repair soon. Really.

Now do you see why I don't want you to tour my closets? I wouldn't want to become known as "Patsy, she who fizzles out." Or Patsy the Fizzler. Or Patsy Fizzes. Unfortunately, I'm not Patsy the Zealous.

I don't know what needs mending in your life, but I'm aware of some broken areas in my own that need repair. May Baruch, a gentleman who aligned his head and his heart, his energy and his determination and who left an indelible mark, inspire us to go and do likewise.

And remember the goldsmiths and perfumers, who were willing to set aside what they were comfortable with to do what needed to be done. The same goes for us when it comes to finding healing. Sometimes we have to look into places we aren't really comfortable looking into!

And don't forget Shallum, who was defined as a man who worked with his daughters, but he was more complex than that—and so are we.

Lord, we often grow weary. Revive us, we pray, until our jobs are done and we are home safe with you.

HEART MENDERS

Are you a worker? Where do you expend most of your energy? Are you a finisher or a fizzler? What area of your life are you willing to have mended? When will you begin?

NEXT

How did a lifetime servant rise up to become a powerful leader? Let's find out.

CHAPTER FIFTEEN

Say a Little Prayer

TO DO.

Read Nehemiah 13:6–9.

I think Nehemiah wore kneepads—that or he had king-size calluses on his kneecaps—because he sure was a praying man. He prayed during crises, he prayed during attacks, he prayed during good times, and he prayed during the discipline of his people.

If we divided the Book of Nehemiah in half, we would find that the first section covers Jerusalem's rebuilding and the last half explores the people's rebuilding. The second half was necessary to keep the first half intact. The finest work in the hands of careless folks never lasts long.

Once we lived in a neighborhood where a rental

home had been renovated and then was leased to a family that appeared to have a reckless lifestyle. The police made regular visits to settle disputes while the property accumulated stuff—mechanical thingam-abobs, vehicles in varying degrees of depreciation, and an array of rather vicious-looking animals. These belongings detracted from the home's curb appeal.

Six months after moving in, the troop that lived there disappeared during the night. I heard tell they had up and robbed a bank and were on the lam; others claimed they had made a hasty departure to stay ahead of the bill collectors. Whatever the case, the once charming home now looked tattered. Broken windows, hanging doors, askew shutters, and tread-marked lawn were the results of folks not prepared to handle their responsibilities.

The opposite was true of Nehemiah. Unlike my rowdy neighbors, this exemplary leader didn't go on the lam from responsibility but met problems head-on. He prayed his way out of a castle, past enemy attacks, and right into people problems and out again. That last difficulty can really throw a person. We expect enemies to be irksome, but it's jarring when our own folks are being irresponsible.

Actually, I find that people issues fill a great deal of my prayer time, how about you?

Remember Me . . .

Nehemiah had to take some strong stands with his people and seemed always to end his righteous skirmishes with this prayer: "Remember me for this, O my God . . ."

"Remember me for this." What do you want to be remembered for before the Lord? Loving service, wise decisions, righteous stands, passionate faith, or all of the above? I don't think Nehemiah prayed because he was a fine leader, but he was a fine leader because he prayed. And the results of his commitment to talk with the only One who could truly help him, or change him, or protect him, was that he became a man of loving service, wise decisions, righteous stands, and passionate faith.

Like Nehemiah, my friend Lana Bateman knows the value of a strong prayer life. People who don't even know her are drawn to her soothing presence. I asked her to be my traveling companion as I journeyed around the country to speak at the Women of Faith Conferences. I knew I would be enriched to have someone with such a passionate prayer life with me. In addition, Lana can be a lot of fun.

By the time Lana took her third trip with me, the other speakers wanted to adopt her. They were impressed with her prayer life, which was especially evident when she interceded for us in the green room before sessions. Soon after, Lana was invited to be the Women of Faith chaplain. She spends time in the

Word, on her knees, seeking counsel from God and doing battle against the enemy on behalf of others.

Lost . . . and Found

I don't believe we're all called to a full-time ministry of intercession, but I do believe we're all called to be on full-time speaking terms with the Lord God of the heavens. I find I stray if I don't pray. It's just that simple. Without that personal connection and accountability, I lose my way. No wonder he calls us sheep. No wonder we need a Shepherd. Ask baa-baad Eliashib.

Nehemiah made a trip back to the Persian palace, but after a stint with the king, he asked permission to return once again to Jerusalem to see how the city was faring. He had left things in good order, with the walls, the gates, the doors, and the towers all repaired. The leadership had been reestablished, and the people were on their faces before the Lord.

But when Nehemiah arrived, he found that Eliashib had prepared a room for Tobiah in the courts of the house of God. Hello-o-o, Eliashib! What were you thinking? Tobiah was Nehemiah's and Jerusalem's enemy. He not only had opposed the rebuilding, but he also openly had taunted their efforts. And now he lived inside the court of the Lord? No wonder Nehemiah proclaimed his displeasure and then threw all of Tobiah's household goods out of the room. Then Nehemiah ordered the rooms to be cleansed.

If we're not watchful, we can do the same thing as Eliashib. We make room for heart trouble when we indulge wrong relationships, excuse unsavory behavior, or entertain the enemy at the cost of truth. But when we pray and ask Christ to come into all the rooms of our heart, he sets things right, throws out the junk, and graciously cleanses the rooms.

The Good Shepherd

Yes, Eliashib was a baa-baad sheep, but he had a Good Shepherd . . . so do we. We are told in the Gospel of John, "The sheep hear his voice, and he calls his own sheep by name, and leads them out. When he puts forth all his own, he goes before them, and the sheep follow him because they know his voice" (John 10:3–4).

No thrill matches hearing the Shepherd say our name, and no joy touches the experience of hearing his voice as we follow. I'm surprised we have to be reminded to talk to him . . . but I do. *Baa.*

As I was writing this chapter, the phone on my desk rang. My sister was calling from Florida to tell me our mom, an Alzheimer's patient, suddenly was having lucid moments. Would I like to talk to her?

I hadn't spoken with my mom for many months because she was incapable of understanding what a telephone was much less carry on a conversation.

Elizabeth wheeled Mom to the phone, and I heard my mother say, "Hello, who is this?"

My heart beat faster at the sound of her dear voice. A voice is such an intimate part of a person, and I found myself flooded with joy and loneliness all at the same time. I hadn't realized how much I had missed the warmth of her words. We talked for ten minutes, with me repeating myself over and over in an attempt to speak through her 80 percent hearing loss. I sang to her several of her favorite hymns, hoping she would remember them.

At one point I said, "Mom, I love you."

She heard that. "Oh, thank you, I love you, too. I haven't talked to you in a long time," she said matter-of-factly.

"Yes, Mom," I answered. "It's been far too long."

I wonder if the Lord doesn't speak to us over and over again in an attempt to converse through our deafness. Has it been a long time since you've talked with him? Far too long? I bet if we'd stop right now and listen, really listen, we'd hear him say, "I love you."

Dear Shepherd, that our bleating prayers matter to you causes us joy. We sheepishly confess our need to have you cleanse our hearts. Thank you for hearing us, for loving us, and for calling us by name.

HEART MENDERS

Do you keep a prayer notebook? If not, try one for a month. Jot down the names of the people you want to remember (including one enemy). You could even add photos. Then devote yourself to covering each person in prayer. At the end of every week, record how you feel about these people and if you've noted any specific answers to your requests.

NEXT

Comforters aren't just something to put on your bed. They can come in many forms.

CHAPTER SIXTEEN

Comfort Ye My People

TO DO.
─────────────

Read Nehemiah 2:17; 18.

If you were to tour the little desert hideaway where Les and I take refuge out of Michigan's fierce winter, you would find it pillow-laden. I just counted, and on our couch and love seat reside thirteen large- to medium-sized pillows. We find it visually inviting and physically comforting, and we hope our guests do as well. We don't just sit down on our couches; we dive backward into the billowing environment and snuggle down into the pillows. Of course, getting out of them is a little challenging once you're underarm-deep in fluff.

If you continued the tour (once you wrested yourself free of the couch pillows), you would come upon towers of pillows in our bedroom. Actually, there are only six, but they're stacked in sets of three. And if you're visually astute, you would notice that one pillow tower is taller than the other. You see, Les likes bulging, substantive pillows to sleep on while I prefer slender, wimpy ones, which leaves my side of the bedding several degrees short of lining up with his. Les's full pillows hurt my neck, and my wimpy ones annoy the daylights out of him. But give us our own pillows and we sleep like babes.

What comforts you? When I was a kid, my grandmother had a feather-filled comforter spread across her aging mattress, and I loved to sleep on it, although I seldom was allowed to. But the memories of when I did are still comforting to me.

Even some foods fill me with childhood memories that I find comforting. In fact, if I were to list my comfort foods, it would look like a week's shopping list for a sizable family. For instance, you know those packages of individually boxed cereals from which you can select half a dozen choices? I love those. Also, peach cobblers emotionally transport me to Kentucky and our wonderful southern relatives. Banana pudding with vanilla wafers piled high with meringue (yum) takes me back into my mom's kitchen.

When Les wants to return to his northern Michigan roots for identification and comfort, he'll eat diced beets mixed with sweet peas tossed in mayonnaise, chocolate cake with peanut butter frosting,

Finnish pastries, and fish eggs (eek). Different things comfort different folks.

A Place of Comfort

The Word of God is full of encouragement, whether one is looking for a comforting environment or a nurturing meal. Of course, it also has parts that initially are disconcerting as they bring us face-to-face with the reflection of truth. But the end result is comfort when that truth has been worked into our character.

I find it interesting that what comforts one may not even speak to another. I have on a number of occasions come across a verse that took on significant meaning for me and in my zeal shared it with friends who listened with interest but obviously weren't moved or impressed. Likewise they have come to me aglow with revelation, but alas, it was their moment not mine.

Perhaps in stepping through the Book of Nehemiah with me, the thoughts I've emphasized weren't what stood out to you. In your own reading, the Spirit of God may have pressed other insights or words into your heart to instruct, direct, or comfort you. I love the Spirit's personalization of God's Word. Even the thought that he works with us so specifically is comforting.

Nehemiah obviously found comfort in hearing from the Lord and then responding to his direction because we watch Nehemiah go from a mourning servant (Neh. 1:4) to a rejoicing leader (Neh. 8:10). And we see Nehemiah extend the Lord's comfort to his people by sharing how God made a way for Nehemiah to come to them. They were not only comforted, but they were also inspired to rise up and build (Neh. 2:17–18).

Don't Get Too Comfortable . . .

A dear mentor used to tell me, "God doesn't comfort us just to make us comfortable, but he comforts us that we might comfort others." Scripture puts it thus: "Praise be to the God and Father of our Lord Jesus Christ, the Father of compassion and the God of all comfort, who comforts us in all our troubles, so that we can comfort those in any trouble with the comfort we ourselves have received from God" (2 Cor. 1:3–4 NIV). Comfort is a condition and an admonition. Nehemiah understood that (Neh. 1:5). And may we take that message to heart. In whatever ways God brings comfort to you, mending your heart from the events that have shattered it, remember that, in turn, you can bring comfort to other battered hearts.

A close friend who was in the midst of marital agony was trying to decide if she should ask her husband to stay elsewhere until he received some much-needed help. Some friends were aghast at her consideration while others prodded her on. Feeling as though she had come to a crossroads on her long, dusty journey, she assessed her broken heart and

149

cried out to God for guidance. The verse he brought to mind went deep into her ache: "For in the time of trouble he shall hide me in his pavilion: in the secret of his tabernacle shall he hide me . . ." (Ps. 27:5 KJV). She said it was as if God gathered her up and spoke comforting peace. She realized she wasn't alone and that the Lord would protect and direct her, showing her the road to take through this difficult time.

When Nehemiah interceded for his people, realizing the difficult road ahead of them, he reminded God of his promise. "If you return to Me and keep My commandments and do them, though those of you who have been scattered were in the most remote part of the heavens, I will gather them from there and will bring them to the place where I have chosen to cause My name to dwell" (Neh. 1:9).

We live in a broken world where we all long to be gathered in the comforting arms of our God—the married and the unmarried, the old and the young.

Recently I read in *Southern Living* magazine a side note regarding the tragedy that struck Texas A&M University a few years ago. The students were following a yearly tradition of building a bonfire out of a tower of wood to display their fiery determination to beat their football rivals, the University of Texas. But when the tower toppled, it ended twelve lives and changed countless others forever.

Later that year, when A&M played against UT again, the memories of the accident hung heavy over the stadium like rain-filled clouds. Despite the years of pranks that the two schools' students had played on each other, during halftime something unexpected happened. The fierce competitors of the Aggies set aside competition for compassion. The University of Texas touched their team flags to the ground and raised their opponent's banners high as their band played "Amazing Grace" and then, in a hushed stadium, "Taps." For a few holy moments the bowl filled with acknowledgment of loss and the desire to comfort the grieving.

We never know whom the Lord will use to minister to our hurting lives. It just might be our greatest rivals.

Be encouraged, my friends. God understands the harshness and hostility of this broken world, and he wants to wrap us in his comforting love whether that is through his Word, his people, or his Spirit.

Dear God of all comfort, we acknowledge our need for your tenderness. Our hearts ache, and you are the only One who can meet us in our pain. The realization of who you are, like a down-filled pillow, offers us rest from our striving. Encircle us with your healing presence and ease the pressures that threaten us. We, in return, Lord, will be sensitive to the lost, the confused, the hurting, and will reach out to them with your gentle touch.

HEART MENDERS

When was the last time you felt God's comfort? What verse(s) have brought you a sense of his nearness? Whom have you comforted?

NEXT

Is that music I hear in the distance? It's a sweet melody, like praise . . .

CHAPTER SEVENTEEN

Songs of Healing

TO DO.

Read Nehemiah 12:27–43.

This book began out of my own personal need to heal. Somehow I thought by my age anything broken inside me would be fixed. Instead, I'm learning that healing and journey are synonymous, and that as long as there is breath in my body there will also be something that needs mending. It's the human condition. That makes sense to me because for a long time I looked for people who had pulled their acts together, but I kept finding other fractured folks who, like me, were in need of repair.

So am I suggesting that all we can hope for in this life is a slightly improved version of our original design?

Perhaps. I guess it depends on what kind of effort and dedication we're willing to put into the journey.

I've seen some amazing changes in people who wholeheartedly followed Christ. They followed him like disciples to the mountaintops and followed him like servants into the valleys. They, like Nehemiah, were cupbearers who drank, with devotion and dignity, the cup he poured them. They were the ones whose sanity stayed intact during the press and whose faith wasn't jarred loose by difficult people. They stepped out of their comfort zones and, if necessary, into the line of fire. They prepared for the enemy so as not to be ambushed by lies, and they committed their minds to Scriptures and their hearts to Christ.

And, honey, I ain't they nor am I there. Oh, I've made progress because I love the Lord and his Word. I've visited a few mountaintops, and I certainly am acquainted with valleys. (Although I think I might have been dragged through a few rather than following willingly.) While my sanity at best is sketchy, I'm grateful for any rendering at this juncture. I confess difficult people still have a way of rattling my bars, and I'm fairly antsy about firing lines.

The good news is I don't have to search to find areas I can improve on. For instance, I'd like to be one who regularly fills my water jar at the well of our Lord, that I might pour out grace to others with my words. I'd like to take servanthood on the road, but first I need to offer it more freely in my own home. I want to grow into a Nehemiah, a Christlike servant, who genuinely and generously loves God's people.

God is a God of grace, and he doesn't want us frantically striving to know him. Yet he does want a relationship with us, which means we have to do more than show up. We can do nothing to qualify—Christ did that on our behalf—but we can be responsive to who he is and what he asks of us.

Let the Work Begin

So where to begin? I think I'll begin in the beginning. No, not the beginning of time, silly, the beginning of the book, with a servant's response, remember? If not, let's review the steps to jog our memories.

We can respond to God by, first, sitting down. That I can do. And when you think about it, that's all Jesus asks of us—what we can do. Begin wherever you are and take the next obvious step in your journey.

Second, we need to weep. Not all tears are from sadness; some are from pure joy. Like hearing the sound of your mother's voice or hearing God speak your name. Don't resist authentic emotions. They are designed that we might feel life and express a myriad of sentiments, including sadness and joy.

Third, we need to mourn. Even though we all must mourn our losses, grieving does have an end. It is a season, not a permanent lodging; you won't have to have your mail sent there. The loss may always be with you, but the pain eases. Honest.

Fourth, we must fast. Giving up is often the first

step in growing up. Denial isn't natural, but it's important to the vitality of our existence. Otherwise we risk becoming self-indulgent dolts.

Fifth, we must pray. Imagine, us on speaking terms with the Lord. He is the only One I know with shoulders broad enough to carry all that weighs me down. And kneeling down in his presence lifts me up. Perhaps that's why we're instructed to pray without ceasing. The Lord *always* has our best interest in mind.

And that's good reason to celebrate. Speaking of which, another part of mending our hearts is relearning how to enter into jubilation. Remember in the opening of this book I said we would enter into a victory celebration? Well, it's time.

Let's Celebrate

Near the end of the Book of Nehemiah the leaders prepared to dedicate the wall and all it represented. They called in the dignitaries (the Levites or priests) that the people might celebrate with gladness and hymns of thanksgiving. Musical accompaniment was arranged, using cymbals, harps, and lyres. The singers were invited, and two great choirs were formed. The choirs met on top of the wall with one choir proceeding in one direction and the other choir walking around the opposite way, encircling the city in praise. The singers sang, sacrifices were offered, and the people rejoiced because God gave them great joy. Jerusalem's joy was heard from afar.

We, too, have reasons to rejoice. We, like Jerusalem, have been in a rebuilding program, and even though our walls may still need some spackling, a stone here or there, and some additional mortar, we are beginning to feel the security and strength that rebuilding brings. The gate hinges may require some WD-40, but our thoughts are improving as we lead out negative thoughts and guide in healthy ones. We've raised some standards (towers), and God's principles give us something to aspire to. They stand tall, and so shall we, as we deliberately guard the truth. And what joy when we open the door to the Lord's knock, and he enters in to meet with us. As we sit at his well, he quenches our thirst in a way nothing else ever has.

When we enter the inevitable valleys, we will not fear, for we've been reassured of his ongoing presence and his overcoming power. And whether we kneel in the valley or on a mountaintop, he leans in to hear our voice and to whisper his love to us.

Perhaps one of the songs we sing should be "Onward Christian Soldiers," as we rise up together as workers and warriors in Jesus' name. Hallelujah!

Remember, a good round of praise enhances our attitudes, raises our spirits, and establishes our feet on solid ground. Praise will hold us in good stead as we travel through this broken world and experience the ongoing mending of our hearts.

We want our joy to be heard from afar. So let's proceed with expectancy, wearing a servant's sandals while we rise to our royal call.

Mended Walls

One of my favorite aspects of Nehemiah's rebuilding program is that the wall took fifty-two days to complete. That's amazing. After a century and a half of lying in dusty ruins, a city was encircled with stone, mortar, and God's love in a matter of days.

I have to believe that if Jerusalem could be brought from such a stony waste place to a thriving city resounding with godly praises, we, too, can experience significant change in our lives in a short time. Many changes, of course, will be of greater duration, but progress is sister to hope.

The Bible is full of time frames that surprise us. For instance, the Flood of Genesis came after forty days of rain. That's just a little more than five weeks; yet the world's geography was reshaped in a matter of days. Jesus' public ministry was only three years—three years that eternally changed the course of history. For three days—count them, one, two, three—Jesus lay in the grave, and on the third day, rigor mortis was defeated by righteousness, and Jesus reigns forever.

From death to life, from darkness to light, from hatred to love, from brokenness to healing—these are Scriptures' hope-filled themes. We can turn away from the darker expressions of our existence and walk the other way; it's our choice. Let's choose life. Let's choose light. Let's choose love. Let's choose healing. Let's choose today.

Songwriter of our Souls, press your music into our spirits that we might daily sing an anthem of praise. O, Lord God of heaven, may the melody from our hearts please you and bless you. We will be careful always to acknowledge you within the gates of our existence. Remember us and our mending hearts with favor. Amen.

HEART MENDERS

Select a theme song for your life that portrays your heart's longing. Commit the words to memory, and sing, sing, sing.

THE BOOK OF
NEHEMIAH

1 ¹The words of Nehemiah the son of Hacaliah. Now it happened in the month Chislev, in the twentieth year, while I was in Susa the capital, ²that Hanani, one of my brothers, and some men from Judah came; and I asked them concerning the Jews who had escaped and had survived the captivity, and about Jerusalem.

³They said to me, "The remnant there in the province who survived the captivity are in great distress and reproach, and the wall of Jerusalem is broken down and its gates are burned with fire."

⁴When I heard these words, I sat down and wept and mourned for days; and I was fasting and praying before the God of heaven. ⁵I said,

"I beseech You, O LORD God of heaven, the great and awesome God, who preserves the covenant and loving kindness for those who love Him and keep His commandments, ⁶let Your ear now be attentive and Your eyes open to hear the prayer of Your servant which I am praying before You now, day and night, on behalf of the sons of Israel Your servants, confessing the sins of the sons of Israel which we have sinned against You; I and my father's house have sinned. [7]"We have acted very corruptly against You and have not kept the commandments, nor the statutes, nor the ordinances which You commanded Your servant Moses.

[8]"Remember the word which You commanded Your servant Moses, saying, 'If you are unfaithful I will scatter you among the peoples; [9]but if you return to Me and keep My commandments and do them, though those of you who have been scattered were in the most remote part of the heavens, I will gather them from there and will bring them to the place where I have chosen to cause My name to dwell.'

[10]"They are Your servants and Your people whom You redeemed by Your great power and by Your strong hand.

[11]"O Lord, I beseech You, may Your ear be attentive to the prayer of Your servant and the prayer of Your servants who delight to revere Your name, and make Your servant successful today and grant him com-

passion before this man." Now I was the cupbearer to the king.

2 [1]And it came about in the month Nisan, in the twentieth year of King Artaxerxes, that wine was before him, and I took up the wine and gave it to the king. Now I had not been sad in his presence. [2]So the king said to me, "Why is your face sad though you are not sick? This is nothing but sadness of heart."

Then I was very much afraid. [3]I said to the king, "Let the king live forever. Why should my face not be sad when the city, the place of my fathers' tombs, lies desolate and its gates have been consumed by fire?"

[4]Then the king said to me, "What would you request?"

So I prayed to the God of heaven. [5]I said to the king, "If it please the king, and if your servant has found favor before you, send me to Judah, to the city of my fathers' tombs, that I may rebuild it."

[6]Then the king said to me, the queen sitting beside him,

"How long will your journey be, and when will you return?" So it pleased the king to send me, and I gave him a definite time.

[7]And I said to the king, "If it please the king, let letters be given me for the governors of the provinces beyond the River, that they may allow me to pass through until I come to Judah, [8]and a letter to Asaph the keeper of the king's forest, that he may give me timber to make beams for the gates of the fortress which is by the temple, for the wall of the city and for the house to which I will go." And the king granted them to me because the good hand of my God was on me. [9]Then I came to the governors of the provinces beyond the River and gave them the king's letters. Now the king had sent with me officers of the army and horsemen.

[10]When Sanballat the Horonite and Tobiah the Ammonite official heard about it, it was very displeasing to them that someone had come to seek the welfare of the sons of Israel.

[11]So I came to Jerusalem and was there three days. [12]And I arose in the night, I and a few men with me. I did not tell anyone what my God was putting into my mind to do for Jerusalem and there was no animal with me except the animal on which I was riding.

[13]So I went out at night by the Valley Gate in the direction of the Dragon's Well and on to the Refuse Gate, inspecting the walls of Jerusalem which were broken down and its gates which were consumed by fire. [14]Then I passed on to the Fountain Gate and the King's Pool, but there was no place for my mount to pass. [15]So I went up at night by the ravine and inspected the wall. Then I entered the Valley Gate again and returned. [16]The officials did not know where I had gone or what I had done; nor had I as yet told the Jews, the priests, the nobles, the officials or the rest who did the work.

[17]Then I said to them, "You see the bad situation we are in, that Jerusalem is desolate and

its gates burned by fire. Come, let us rebuild the wall of Jerusalem so that we will no longer be a reproach." [18]I told them how the hand of my God had been favorable to me and also about the king's words which he had spoken to me. Then they said, "Let us arise and build." So they put their hands to the good work.

[19]But when Sanballat the Horonite and Tobiah the Ammonite official, and Geshem the Arab heard it, they mocked us and despised us and said, "What is this thing you are doing? Are you rebelling against the king?"

[20]So I answered them and said to them, "The God of heaven will give us success; therefore we His servants will arise and build, but you have no portion, right or memorial in Jerusalem."

3 [1]Then Eliashib the high priest arose with his brothers the priests and built the Sheep Gate; they consecrated it and hung its doors. They conse-crated the wall to the Tower of the Hundred and the Tower of Hananel. [2]Next to him the men of Jericho built, and next to them Zaccur the son of Imri built.

[3]Now the sons of Hassenaah built the Fish Gate; they laid its beams and hung its doors with its bolts and bars. [4]Next to them Meremoth the son of Uriah the son of Hakkoz made repairs. And next to him Meshullam the son of Berechiah the son of Meshezabel made repairs. And next to him Zadok the son of Baana also made repairs. [5]Moreover, next to him the Tekoites made repairs, but their nobles did not support the work of their masters.

[6]Joiada the son of Paseah and Meshullam the son of Besodeiah repaired the Old Gate; they laid its beams and hung its doors with its bolts and its bars. [7]Next to them Mela-tiah the Gibeonite and Jadon the Meronothite, the men of Gibeon and of Mizpah, also made repairs for the official seat of the governor of the province beyond the River. [8]Next to him

Uzziel the son of Harhaiah of the goldsmiths made repairs. And next to him Hananiah, one of the perfumers, made repairs, and they restored Jerusalem as far as the Broad Wall. [9]Next to them Rephaiah the son of Hur, the official of half the district of Jerusalem, made repairs. [10]Next to them Jedaiah the son of Harumaph made repairs opposite his house. And next to him Hattush the son of Hashabneiah made repairs. [11]Malchijah the son of Harim and Hasshub the son of Pahath-moab repaired another section and the Tower of Furnaces. [12]Next to him Shallum the son of Hallohesh, the official of half the district of Jerusalem, made repairs, he and his daughters.

[13]Hanun and the inhabitants of Zanoah repaired the Valley Gate. They built it and hung its doors with its bolts and its bars, and a thousand cubits of the wall to the Refuse Gate.

[14]Malchijah the son of Rechab, the official of the district of Beth-haccherem repaired the Refuse Gate. He built it and hung its doors with its bolts and its bars.

[15]Shallum the son of Colhozeh, the official of the district of Mizpah, repaired the Fountain Gate. He built it, covered it and hung its doors with its bolts and its bars, and the wall of the Pool of Shelah at the king's garden as far as the steps that descend from the city of David. [16]After him Nehemiah the son of Azbuk, official of half the district of Beth-zur, made repairs as far as a point opposite the tombs of David, and as far as the artificial pool and the house of the mighty men.

[17]After him the Levites carried out repairs under Rehum the son of Bani. Next to him Hashabiah, the official of half the district of Keilah, carried out repairs for his district. [18]After him their brothers carried out repairs under Bavvai the son of Henadad, official of the other half of the district of Keilah. [19]Next to him Ezer the son of Jeshua, the official of Mizpah, repaired another section in front of the ascent of the armory at the Angle. [20]After

him Baruch the son of Zabbai zealously repaired another section, from the Angle to the doorway of the house of Eliashib the high priest. [21]After him Meremoth the son of Uriah the son of Hakkoz repaired another section, from the doorway of Eliashib's house even as far as the end of his house.

[22]After him the priests, the men of the valley, carried out repairs. [23]After them Benjamin and Hasshub carried out repairs in front of their house. After them Azariah the son of Maaseiah, son of Ananiah, carried out repairs beside his house. [24]After him Binnui the son of Henadad repaired another section, from the house of Azariah as far as the Angle and as far as the corner. [25]Palal the son of Uzai made repairs in front of the Angle and the tower projecting from the upper house of the king, which is by the court of the guard. After him Pedaiah the son of Parosh made repairs. [26]The temple servants living in Ophel made repairs as far as the front of the Water Gate toward the east and the projecting tower. [27]After

them the Tekoites repaired another section in front of the great projecting tower and as far as the wall of Ophel.

[28]Above the Horse Gate the priests carried out repairs, each in front of his house. [29]After them Zadok the son of Immer carried out repairs in front of his house. And after him Shemaiah the son of Shecaniah, the keeper of the East Gate, carried out repairs. [30]After him Hananiah the son of Shelemiah, and Hanun the sixth son of Zalaph, repaired another section. After him Meshullam the son of Berechiah carried out repairs in front of his own quarters. [31]After him Malchijah, one of the goldsmiths, carried out repairs as far as the house of the temple servants and of the merchants, in front of the Inspection Gate and as far as the upper room of the corner. [32]Between the upper room of the corner and the Sheep Gate the goldsmiths and the merchants carried out repairs.

4 [1]Now it came about that when Sanballat heard that we

were rebuilding the wall, he became furious and very angry and mocked the Jews. ²He spoke in the presence of his brothers and the wealthy men of Samaria and said, "What are these feeble Jews doing? Are they going to restore it for themselves? Can they offer sacrifices? Can they finish in a day? Can they revive the stones from the dusty rubble even the burned ones?"

³Now Tobiah the Ammonite was near him and he said, "Even what they are building if a fox should jump on it, he would break their stone wall down!"

⁴Hear, O our God, how we are despised! Return their reproach on their own heads and give them up for plunder in a land of captivity. ⁵Do not forgive their iniquity and let not their sin be blotted out before You, for they have demoralized the builders.

⁶So we built the wall and the whole wall was joined together to half its height, for the people had a mind to work.

⁷Now when Sanballat, Tob-iah, the Arabs, the Ammonites and the Ashdodites heard that the repair of the walls of Jerusalem went on, and that the breaches began to be closed, they were very angry. ⁸All of them conspired together to come and fight against Jerusalem and to cause a disturbance in it. ⁹But we prayed to our God, and because of them we set up a guard against them day and night.

¹⁰Thus in Judah it was said, "The strength of the burden bearers is failing, Yet there is much rubbish; And we ourselves are unable To rebuild the wall."

¹¹Our enemies said, "They will not know or see until we come among them, kill them and put a stop to the work."

¹²When the Jews who lived near them came and told us ten times, "They will come up against us from every place where you may turn,"

¹³then I stationed men in the lowest parts of the space behind the wall, the exposed places, and I stationed the people in families with their swords,

spears and bows. ¹⁴When I saw their fear, I rose and spoke to the nobles, the officials and the rest of the people: "Do not be afraid of them; remember the Lord who is great and awesome, and fight for your brothers, your sons, your daughters, your wives and your houses."

¹⁵When our enemies heard that it was known to us, and that God had frustrated their plan, then all of us returned to the wall, each one to his work.

¹⁶From that day on, half of my servants carried on the work while half of them held the spears, the shields, the bows and the breastplates; and the captains were behind the whole house of Judah. ¹⁷Those who were rebuilding the wall and those who carried burdens took their load with one hand doing the work and the other holding a weapon. ¹⁸As for the builders, each wore his sword girded at his side as he built, while the trumpeter stood near me.

¹⁹I said to the nobles, the officials and the rest of the people, "The work is great and extensive, and we are separated on the wall far from one another. ²⁰"At whatever place you hear the sound of the trumpet, rally to us there. Our God will fight for us."

²¹So we carried on the work with half of them holding spears from dawn until the stars appeared. ²²At that time I also said to the people, "Let each man with his servant spend the night within Jerusalem so that they may be a guard for us by night and a laborer by day." ²³So neither I, my brothers, my servants, nor the men of the guard who followed me, none of us removed our clothes, each took his weapon even to the water.

5 ¹Now there was a great outcry of the people and of their wives against their Jewish brothers. ²For there were those who said, "We, our sons and our daughters are many; therefore let us get grain that we may eat and live."

³There were others who said, "We are mortgaging our fields, our vineyards and our houses that we might get grain because of the famine."

⁴Also there were those who said, "We have borrowed money for the king's tax on our fields and our vineyards.

⁵"Now our flesh is like the flesh of our brothers, our children like their children. Yet behold, we are forcing our sons and our daughters to be slaves, and some of our daughters are forced into bondage already, and we are helpless because our fields and vineyards belong to others."

⁶Then I was very angry when I had heard their outcry and these words. ⁷I consulted with myself and contended with the nobles and the rulers and said to them, "You are exacting usury, each from his brother!" Therefore, I held a great assembly against them. ⁸I said to them, "We according to our ability have redeemed our Jewish brothers who were sold to the nations; now would you even sell your brothers that they may be sold to us?" Then they were silent and could not find a word to say.

⁹Again I said, "The thing which you are doing is not good; should you not walk in the fear of our God because of the reproach of the nations, our enemies?

¹⁰"And likewise I, my brothers and my servants are lending them money and grain. Please, let us leave off this usury. ¹¹"Please, give back to them this very day their fields, their vineyards, their olive groves and their houses, also the hundredth part of the money and of the grain, the new wine and the oil that you are exacting from them."

¹²Then they said, "We will give it back and will require nothing from them; we will do exactly as you say." So I called the priests and took an oath from them that they would do according to this promise. ¹³I also shook out the front of my garment and said, "Thus may God shake out every man from his house and from his possessions who does not fulfill this promise; even thus may he be shaken out and emptied."

And all the assembly said, "Amen!" And they praised the LORD. Then the people did according to this promise.

¹⁴Moreover, from the day that I was appointed to be their governor in the land of Judah, from the twentieth year to the thirty-second year of King Artaxerxes, for twelve years, neither I nor my kinsmen have eaten the governor's food allowance. ¹⁵But the former governors who were before me laid burdens on the people and took from them bread and wine besides forty shekels of silver; even their servants domineered the people. But I did not do so because of the fear of God. ¹⁶I also applied myself to the work on this wall; we did not buy any land, and all my servants were gathered there for the work.

¹⁷Moreover, there were at my table one hundred and fifty Jews and officials, besides those who came to us from the nations that were around us. ¹⁸Now that which was prepared for each day was one ox and six choice sheep, also birds were prepared for me; and once in ten days all sorts of wine were furnished in abundance. Yet for all this I did not demand the governor's food allowance, because the servitude was heavy on this people.

¹⁹Remember me, O my God, for good, according to all that I have done for this people.

6 ¹Now when it was reported to Sanballat, Tobiah, to Geshem the Arab and to the rest of our enemies that I had rebuilt the wall, and that no breach remained in it, although at that time I had not set up the doors in the gates, ²then Sanballat and Geshem sent a message to me, saying, "Come, let us meet together at Chephirim in the plain of Ono."

But they were planning to harm me. ³So I sent messengers to them, saying, "I am doing a great work and I cannot come down. Why should the work stop while I leave it and come down to you?" ⁴They sent messages to me four times in this manner, and I answered them in the same way.

⁵Then Sanballat sent his servant to me in the same manner a fifth time with an open letter in his hand. ⁶In it was written,

"It is reported among the nations, and Gashmu says, that you and the Jews are planning to rebel; therefore you are rebuilding the wall. And you are to be their king, according to these reports. [7]You have also appointed prophets to proclaim in Jerusalem concerning you, 'A king is in Judah!' And now it will be reported to the king according to these reports. So come now, let us take counsel together."

[8]Then I sent a message to him saying, "Such things as you are saying have not been done, but you are inventing them in your own mind."

[9]For all of them were trying to frighten us, thinking, "They will become discouraged with the work and it will not be done."

But now, O God, strengthen my hands.

[10]When I entered the house of Shemaiah the son of Delaiah, son of Mehetabel, who was confined at home, he said, "Let us meet together in the house of God, within the temple, and let us close the doors of the temple, for they are coming to kill you, and they are coming to kill you at night."

[11]But I said, "Should a man like me flee? And could one such as I go into the temple to save his life? I will not go in." [12]Then I perceived that surely God had not sent him, but he uttered his prophecy against me because Tobiah and Sanballat had hired him. [13]He was hired for this reason, that I might become frightened and act accordingly and sin, so that they might have an evil report in order that they could reproach me.

[14]Remember, O my God, Tobiah and Sanballat according to these works of theirs, and also Noadiah the prophetess and the rest of the prophets who were trying to frighten me.

[15]So the wall was completed on the twenty-fifth of the month Elul, in fifty-two days. [16]When all our enemies heard of it, and all the nations surrounding us saw it, they lost

171

their confidence; for they recognized that this work had been accomplished with the help of our God.

¹⁷Also in those days many letters went from the nobles of Judah to Tobiah, and Tobiah's letters came to them. ¹⁸For many in Judah were bound by oath to him because he was the son-in-law of Shecaniah the son of Arah, and his son Jehohanan had married the daughter of Meshullam the son of Berechiah. ¹⁹Moreover, they were speaking about his good deeds in my presence and reported my words to him. Then Tobiah sent letters to frighten me.

7 ¹Now when the wall was rebuilt and I had set up the doors, and the gatekeepers and the singers and the Levites were appointed, ²then I put Hanani my brother, and Hananiah the commander of the fortress, in charge of Jerusalem, for he was a faithful man and feared God more than many. ³Then I said to them, "Do not let the gates of Jerusalem be opened until the sun is hot, and while they are standing guard, let them shut and bolt the doors. Also appoint guards from the inhabitants of Jerusalem, each at his post, and each in front of his own house."

⁴Now the city was large and spacious, but the people in it were few and the houses were not built. ⁵Then my God put it into my heart to assemble the nobles, the officials and the people to be enrolled by genealogies. Then I found the book of the genealogy of those who came up first in which I found the following record:

⁶These are the people of the province who came up from the captivity of the exiles whom Nebuchadnezzar the king of Babylon had carried away, and who returned to Jerusalem and Judah, each to his city, ⁷who came with Zerubbabel, Jeshua, Nehemiah, Azariah, Raamiah, Nahamani, Mordecai, Bilshan, Mispereth, Bigvai, Nehum, Baanah. The number of men of the people of Israel:

⁸the sons of Parosh, 2,172;

[9]the sons of Shephatiah, 372;

[10]the sons of Arah, 652;

[11]the sons of Pahath-moab of the sons of Jeshua and Joab, 2,818;

[12]the sons of Elam, 1,254;

[13]the sons of Zattu, 845;

[14]the sons of Zaccai, 760;

[15]the sons of Binnui, 648;

[16]the sons of Bebai, 628;

[17]the sons of Azgad, 2,322;

[18]the sons of Adonikam, 667;

[19]the sons of Bigvai, 2,067;

[20]the sons of Adin, 655;

[21]the sons of Ater, of Hezekiah, 98;

[22]the sons of Hashum, 328;

[23]the sons of Bezai, 324;

[24]the sons of Hariph, 112;

[25]the sons of Gibeon, 95;

[26]the men of Bethlehem and Netophah, 188;

[27]the men of Anathoth, 128;

[28]the men of Beth-azmaveth, 42;

[29]the men of Kiriath-jearim, Chephirah and Beeroth, 743;

[30]the men of Ramah and Geba, 621;

[31]the men of Michmas, 122;

[32]the men of Bethel and Ai, 123;

[33]the men of the other Nebo, 52;

[34]the sons of the other Elam, 1,254;

[35]the sons of Harim, 320;

[36]the men of Jericho, 345;

[37]the sons of Lod, Hadid and Ono, 721;

[38]the sons of Senaah, 3,930.

[39]The priests: the sons of Jedaiah of the house of Jeshua, 973;

[40]the sons of Immer, 1,052;

[41]the sons of Pashhur, 1,247;

[42]the sons of Harim, 1,017.

[43]The Levites: the sons of Jeshua, of Kadmiel, of the sons of Hodevah, 74.

[44]The singers: the sons of Asaph, 148.

[45]The gatekeepers: the sons of Shallum, the sons of Ater, the sons of Talmon, the sons of Akkub, the sons of Hatita, the sons of Shobai, 138.

[46]The temple servants: the sons of Ziha, the sons of Hasupha, the sons of Tabbaoth,

[47]the sons of Keros, the sons of Sia, the sons of Padon,

[48]the sons of Lebana, the sons of Hagaba, the sons of Shalmai,

⁴⁹the sons of Hanan, the sons of Giddel, the sons of Gahar,

⁵⁰the sons of Reaiah, the sons of Rezin, the sons of Nekoda,

⁵¹the sons of Gazzam, the sons of Uzza, the sons of Paseah,

⁵²the sons of Besai, the sons of Meunim, the sons of Nephushesim,

⁵³the sons of Bakbuk, the sons of Hakupha, the sons of Harhur,

⁵⁴the sons of Bazlith, the sons of Mehida, the sons of Harsha,

⁵⁵the sons of Barkos, the sons of Sisera, the sons of Temah,

⁵⁶the sons of Neziah, the sons of Hatipha. ⁵⁷The sons of Solomon's servants: the sons of Sotai, the sons of Sophereth, the sons of Perida,

⁵⁸the sons of Jaala, the sons of Darkon, the sons of Giddel,

⁵⁹the sons of Shephatiah, the sons of Hattil, the sons of Pochereth-hazzebaim, the sons of Amon.

⁶⁰All the temple servants and the sons of Solomon's servants were 392.

⁶¹These were they who came up from Tel-melah, Tel-harsha, Cherub, Addon and Immer; but they could not show their fathers' houses or their descendants, whether they were of Israel:

⁶²the sons of Delaiah, the sons of Tobiah, the sons of Nekoda, 642.

⁶³Of the priests: the sons of Hobaiah, the sons of Hakkoz, the sons of Barzillai, who took a wife of the daughters of Barzillai, the Gileadite, and was named after them.

⁶⁴These searched among their ancestral registration, but it could not be located; therefore they were considered unclean and excluded from the priesthood. ⁶⁵The governor said to them that they should not eat from the most holy things until a priest arose with Urim and Thummim.

⁶⁶The whole assembly together was 42,360, ⁶⁷besides their male and their female servants, of whom there were 7,337; and they had 245 male and female singers. ⁶⁸Their horses were 736; their mules, 245; ⁶⁹their camels, 435; their donkeys, 6,720.

⁷⁰Some from among the

heads of fathers' households gave to the work. The governor gave to the treasury 1,000 gold drachmas, 50 basins, 530 priests' garments. [71]Some of the heads of fathers' households gave into the treasury of the work 20,000 gold drachmas and 2,200 silver minas. [72]That which the rest of the people gave was 20,000 gold drachmas and 2,000 silver minas and priests' garments.

[73]Now the priests, the Levites, the gatekeepers, the singers, some of the people, the temple servants and all Israel, lived in their cities. And when the seventh month came, the sons of Israel were in their cities.

8 [1]And all the people gathered as one man at the square which was in front of the Water Gate, and they asked Ezra the scribe to bring the book of the law of Moses which the LORD had given to Israel.

[2]Then Ezra the priest brought the law before the assembly of men, women and all who could listen with understanding, on the first day of the seventh month. [3]He read from it before the square which was in front of the Water Gate from early morning until midday, in the presence of men and women, those who could understand; and all the people were attentive to the book of the law.

[4]Ezra the scribe stood at a wooden podium which they had made for the purpose. And beside him stood Mattithiah, Shema, Anaiah, Uriah, Hilkiah, and Maaseiah on his right hand; and Pedaiah, Mishael, Malchijah, Hashum, Hashbaddanah, Zechariah and Meshullam on his left hand.

[5]Ezra opened the book in the sight of all the people for he was standing above all the people; and when he opened it, all the people stood up. [6]Then Ezra blessed the LORD the great God. And all the people answered, "Amen, Amen!" while lifting up their hands; then they bowed low and worshiped the LORD with their faces to the ground.

[7]Also Jeshua, Bani, Shere-biah, Jamin, Akkub, Shab-bethai, Hodiah, Maaseiah, Kelita, Azariah, Jozabad, Hanan, Pelaiah, the Levites, explained the law to the people while the people remained in their place. [8]They read from the book, from the law of God, translating to give the sense so that they understood the reading.

[9]Then Nehemiah, who was the governor, and Ezra the priest and scribe, and the Levites who taught the people said to all the people, "This day is holy to the LORD your God; do not mourn or weep." For all the people were weeping when they heard the words of the law.

[10]Then he said to them, "Go, eat of the fat, drink of the sweet, and send portions to him who has nothing prepared; for this day is holy to our Lord. Do not be grieved, for the joy of the LORD is your strength."

[11]So the Levites calmed all the people, saying, "Be still, for the day is holy; do not be grieved."

[12]All the people went away to eat, to drink, to send por-tions and to celebrate a great festival, because they under-stood the words which had been made known to them.

[13]Then on the second day the heads of fathers' households of all the people, the priests and the Levites were gathered to Ezra the scribe that they might gain insight into the words of the law. [14]They found written in the law how the LORD had com-manded through Moses that the sons of Israel should live in booths during the feast of the seventh month. [15]So they pro-claimed and circulated a proclamation in all their cities and in Jerusalem, saying, "Go out to the hills, and bring olive branches and wild olive branches, myrtle branches, palm branches and branches of other leafy trees, to make booths, as it is written."

[16]So the people went out and brought them and made booths for themselves, each on his roof, and in their courts and in the courts of the house of God, and in the square at the

Water Gate and in the square at the Gate of Ephraim. [17]The entire assembly of those who had returned from the captivity made booths and lived in them. The sons of Israel had indeed not done so from the days of Joshua the son of Nun to that day. And there was great rejoicing.

[18]He read from the book of the law of God daily, from the first day to the last day. And they celebrated the feast seven days, and on the eighth day there was a solemn assembly according to the ordinance.

9 [1]Now on the twenty-fourth day of this month the sons of Israel assembled with fasting, in sackcloth and with dirt upon them. [2]The descendants of Israel separated themselves from all foreigners, and stood and confessed their sins and the iniquities of their fathers. [3]While they stood in their place, they read from the book of the law of the LORD their God for a fourth of the day; and for another fourth they con-

fessed and worshiped the LORD their God. [4]Now on the Levites' platform stood Jeshua, Bani, Kadmiel, Shebaniah, Bunni, Sherebiah, Bani and Chenani, and they cried with a loud voice to the LORD their God. [5]Then the Levites, Jeshua, Kadmiel, Bani, Hashabneiah, Sherebiah, Hodiah, Shebaniah and Pethahiah, said, "Arise, bless the LORD your God forever and ever!

O may Your glorious name be blessed And exalted above all blessing and praise! [6]"You alone are the LORD. You have made the heavens, The heaven of heavens with all their host, The earth and all that is on it, The seas and all that is in them. You give life to all of them And the heavenly host bows down before You.

[7]"You are the LORD God, Who chose Abram And brought him out from Ur of the Chaldees, And gave him the name Abraham. [8]"You found his heart faithful before You, And made a covenant with him To give him the land of the

177

Canaanite, Of the Hittite and the Amorite, Of the Perizzite, the Jebusite and the Girgashite To give it to his descendants. And You have fulfilled Your promise, For You are righteous.

⁹"You saw the affliction of our fathers in Egypt, And heard their cry by the Red Sea. ¹⁰"Then You performed signs and wonders against Pharaoh, Against all his servants and all the people of his land; For You knew that they acted arrogantly toward them, And made a name for Yourself as it is this day.

¹¹"You divided the sea before them, So they passed through the midst of the sea on dry ground; And their pursuers You hurled into the depths, Like a stone into raging waters. ¹²"And with a pillar of cloud You led them by day, And with a pillar of fire by night To light for them the way In which they were to go.

¹³"Then You came down on Mount Sinai, And spoke with them from heaven; You gave them just ordinances and true laws, Good statutes and com-mandments. ¹⁴"So You made known to them Your holy sab-bath, And laid down for them commandments, statutes and law, Through Your servant Moses. ¹⁵"You provided bread from heaven for them for their hunger, You brought forth water from a rock for them for their thirst, And You told them to enter in order to possess The land which You swore to give them.

¹⁶"But they, our fathers, acted arrogantly; They became stubborn and would not listen to Your commandments. ¹⁷"They refused to listen, And did not remember Your won-drous deeds which You had performed among them; So they became stubborn and appointed a leader to return to their slavery in Egypt. But You are a God of forgiveness, Gra-cious and compassionate, Slow to anger and abounding in lov-ingkindness; And You did not forsake them. ¹⁸"Even when they made for themselves A calf of molten metal And said, 'This is your God Who brought you up from Egypt,'

And committed great blasphemies,

[19]You, in Your great compassion, Did not forsake them in the wilderness; The pillar of cloud did not leave them by day, To guide them on their way, Nor the pillar of fire by night, to light for them the way in which they were to go. [20]"You gave Your good Spirit to instruct them, Your manna You did not withhold from their mouth, And You gave them water for their thirst.

[21]"Indeed, forty years You provided for them in the wilderness and they were not in want; Their clothes did not wear out, nor did their feet swell.

[22]"You also gave them kingdoms and peoples, And allotted them to them as a boundary. They took possession of the land of Sihon the king of Heshbon And the land of Og the king of Bashan. [23]"You made their sons numerous as the stars of heaven, And You brought them into the land Which You had told their fathers to enter and possess. [24]"So their sons entered and possessed the land. And You subdued before them the inhabitants of the land, the Canaanites, And You gave them into their hand, with their kings and the peoples of the land, To do with them as they desired. [25]"They captured fortified cities and a fertile land. They took possession of houses full of every good thing, Hewn cisterns, vineyards, olive groves, Fruit trees in abundance. So they ate, were filled and grew fat, And reveled in Your great goodness.

[26]"But they became disobedient and rebelled against You, And cast Your law behind their backs And killed Your prophets who had admonished them So that they might return to You, And they committed great blasphemies. [27]"Therefore You delivered them into the hand of their oppressors who oppressed them, But when they cried to You in the time of their distress, You heard from heaven, and according to Your great compassion You gave them deliverers who delivered them from the hand of their oppressors.

²⁸"But as soon as they had rest, they did evil again before You; Therefore You abandoned them to the hand of their enemies, so that they ruled over them. When they cried again to You, You heard from heaven, And many times You rescued them according to Your compassion,

²⁹And admonished them in order to turn them back to Your law. Yet they acted arrogantly and did not listen to Your commandments but sinned against Your ordinances, By which if a man observes them he shall live. And they turned a stubborn shoulder and stiffened their neck, and would not listen. ³⁰"However, You bore with them for many years, And admonished them by Your Spirit through Your prophets, Yet they would not give ear. Therefore You gave them into the hand of the peoples of the lands. ³¹"Nevertheless, in Your great compassion You did not make an end of them or forsake them, For You are a gracious and compassionate God.

³²"Now therefore, our God, the great, the mighty, and the awesome God, who keeps covenant and lovingkindness, Do not let all the hardship seem insignificant before You, Which has come upon us, our kings, our princes, our priests, our prophets, our fathers and on all Your people, From the days of the kings of Assyria to this day. ³³"However, You are just in all that has come upon us; For You have dealt faithfully, but we have acted wickedly. ³⁴"For our kings, our leaders, our priests and our fathers have not kept Your law Or paid attention to Your commandments and Your admonitions with which You have admonished them. ³⁵"But they, in their own kingdom, With Your great goodness which You gave them, With the broad and rich land which You set before them, Did not serve You or turn from their evil deeds.

³⁶"Behold, we are slaves today, And as to the land which You gave to our fathers to eat of its fruit and its bounty, Behold, we are slaves in it. ³⁷"Its abun-

dant produce is for the kings Whom You have set over us because of our sins; They also rule over our bodies And over our cattle as they please, So we are in great distress.

³⁸"Now because of all this We are making an agreement in writing; And on the sealed document are the names of our leaders, our Levites and our priests."

10

¹Now on the sealed document were the names of:

Nehemiah the governor, the son of Hacaliah, and Zedekiah,

²Seraiah, Azariah, Jeremiah, ³Pashhur, Amariah, Malchijah,

⁴Hattush, Shebaniah, Malluch,

⁵Harim, Meremoth, Obadiah,

⁶Daniel, Ginnethon, Baruch, ⁷Meshullam, Abijah, Mijamin,

⁸Maaziah, Bilgai, Shemaiah. These were the priests.

⁹And the Levites: Jeshua the son of Azaniah, Binnui of the sons of Henadad, Kadmiel;

¹⁰also their brothers Shebaniah, Hodiah, Kelita, Pelaiah, Hanan,

¹¹Mica, Rehob, Hashabiah, ¹²Zaccur, Sherebiah, Shebaniah,

¹³Hodiah, Bani, Beninu.

¹⁴The leaders of the people: Parosh, Pahath-moab, Elam, Zattu, Bani,

¹⁵Bunni, Azgad, Bebai, ¹⁶Adonijah, Bigvai, Adin, ¹⁷Ater, Hezekiah, Azzur, ¹⁸Hodiah, Hashum, Bezai, ¹⁹Hariph, Anathoth, Nebai, ²⁰Magpiash, Meshullam, Hezir,

²¹Meshezabel, Zadok, Jaddua, ²²Pelatiah, Hanan, Anaiah, ²³Hoshea, Hananiah, Hasshub,

²⁴Hallohesh, Pilha, Shobek, ²⁵Rehum, Hashabnah, Maaseiah,

²⁶Ahiah, Hanan, Anan, ²⁷Malluch, Harim, Baanah.

²⁸Now the rest of the people, the priests, the Levites, the gatekeepers, the singers, the temple servants and all those who had separated themselves from the peoples of the lands to the law of God, their wives,

their sons and their daughters, all those who had knowledge and understanding, [29]are joining with their kinsmen, their nobles, and are taking on themselves a curse and an oath to walk in God's law, which was given through Moses, God's servant, and to keep and to observe all the commandments of GOD our Lord, and His ordinances and His statutes;

[30]and that we will not give our daughters to the peoples of the land or take their daughters for our sons. [31]As for the peoples of the land who bring wares or any grain on the sabbath day to sell, we will not buy from them on the sabbath or a holy day; and we will forego the crops the seventh year and the exaction of every debt.

[32]We also placed ourselves under obligation to contribute yearly one third of a shekel for the service of the house of our God: [33]for the showbread, for the continual grain offering, for the continual burnt offering, the sabbaths, the new moon, for the appointed times, for the holy things and for the sin

offerings to make atonement for Israel, and all the work of the house of our God.

[34]Likewise we cast lots for the supply of wood among the priests, the Levites and the people so that they might bring it to the house of our God, according to our fathers' households, at fixed times annually, to burn on the altar of the LORD our God, as it is written in the law;

[35]and that they might bring the first fruits of our ground and the first fruits of all the fruit of every tree to the house of the LORD annually,

[36]and bring to the house of our God the firstborn of our sons and of our cattle, and the firstborn of our herds and our flocks as it is written in the law, for the priests who are ministering in the house of our God.

[37]We will also bring the first of our dough, our contributions, the fruit of every tree, the new wine and the oil to the priests at the chambers of the house of our God, and the tithe of our ground to the Levites, for the Levites are they

who receive the tithes in all the rural towns. [38]The priest, the son of Aaron, shall be with the Levites when the Levites receive tithes, and the Levites shall bring up the tenth of the tithes to the house of our God, to the chambers of the storehouse. [39]For the sons of Israel and the sons of Levi shall bring the contribution of the grain, the new wine and the oil to the chambers; there are the utensils of the sanctuary, the priests who are ministering, the gatekeepers and the singers. Thus we will not neglect the house of our God.

11 [1]Now the leaders of the people lived in Jerusalem, but the rest of the people cast lots to bring one out of ten to live in Jerusalem, the holy city, while nine-tenths remained in the other cities. [2]And the people blessed all the men who volunteered to live in Jerusalem.

[3]Now these are the heads of the provinces who lived in Jerusalem, but in the cities of Judah each lived on his own property in their cities—the Israelites, the priests, the Levites, the temple servants and the descendants of Solomon's servants. [4]Some of the sons of Judah and some of the sons of Benjamin lived in Jerusalem.

From the sons of Judah: Athaiah the son of Uzziah, the son of Zechariah, the son of Amariah, the son of Shephatiah, the son of Mahalalel, of the sons of Perez; [5]and Maaseiah the son of Baruch, the son of Col-hozeh, the son of Hazaiah, the son of Adaiah, the son of Joiarib, the son of Zechariah, the son of the Shilonite. [6]All the sons of Perez who lived in Jerusalem were 468 able men.

[7]Now these are the sons of Benjamin: Sallu the son of Meshullam, the son of Joed, the son of Pedaiah, the son of Kolaiah, the son of Maaseiah, the son of Ithiel, the son of Jeshaiah; [8]and after him Gabbai and Sallai, 928. [9]Joel the son of Zichri was their overseer, and Judah the son of Hassenuah was second in command of the city.

¹⁰From the priests: Jedaiah the son of Joiarib, Jachin, ¹¹Seraiah the son of Hilkiah, the son of Meshullam, the son of Zadok, the son of Meraioth, the son of Ahitub, the leader of the house of God, ¹²and their kinsmen who performed the work of the temple, 822; and Adaiah the son of Jeroham, the son of Pelaliah, the son of Amzi, the son of Zechariah, the son of Pashhur, the son of Malchijah, ¹³and his kinsmen, heads of fathers' households, 242; and Amashsai the son of Azarel, the son of Ahzai, the son of Meshillemoth, the son of Immer, ¹⁴and their brothers, valiant warriors, 128. And their overseer was Zabdiel, the son of Haggedolim.

¹⁵Now from the Levites: Shemaiah the son of Hasshub, the son of Azrikam, the son of Hashabiah, the son of Bunni; ¹⁶and Shabbethai and Jozabad, from the leaders of the Levites, who were in charge of the outside work of the house of God; ¹⁷and Mattaniah the son of Mica, the son of Zabdi, the son of Asaph, who was the leader in beginning the thanksgiving at prayer, and Bakbukiah, the second among his brethren; and Abda the son of Shammua, the son of Galal, the son of Jeduthun. ¹⁸All the Levites in the holy city were 284.

¹⁹Also the gatekeepers, Akkub, Talmon and their brethren who kept watch at the gates, were 172.

²⁰The rest of Israel, of the priests and of the Levites, were in all the cities of Judah, each on his own inheritance.

²¹But the temple servants were living in Ophel, and Ziha and Gishpa were in charge of the temple servants.

²²Now the overseer of the Levites in Jerusalem was Uzzi the son of Bani, the son of Hashabiah, the son of Mattaniah, the son of Mica, from the sons of Asaph, who were the singers for the service of the house of God. ²³For there was a commandment from the king concerning them and a firm regulation for the song leaders day by day.

24Pethahiah the son of Meshezabel, of the sons of Zerah the son of Judah, was the king's representative in all matters concerning the people.

25Now as for the villages with their fields, some of the sons of Judah lived in Kiriatharba and its towns, in Dibon and its towns, and in Jekabzeel and its villages, 26and in Jeshua, in Moladah and Beth-pelet, 27and in Hazar-shual, in Beersheba and its towns, 28and in Ziklag, in Meconah and in its towns, 29and in En-rimmon, in Zorah and in Jarmuth, 30Zanoah, Adullam, and their villages, Lachish and its fields, Azekah and its towns. So they encamped from Beersheba as far as the valley of Hinnom.

31The sons of Benjamin also lived from Geba onward, at Michmash and Aija, at Bethel and its towns, 32at Anathoth, Nob, Ananiah, 33Hazor, Ramah, Gittaim, 34Hadid, Zeboim, Neballat, 35Lod and Ono, the valley of craftsmen.

36From the Levites, some divisions in Judah belonged to Benjamin.

12 1Now these are the priests and the Levites who came up with Zerubbabel the son of Shealtiel, and Jeshua: Seraiah, Jeremiah, Ezra,

2Amariah, Malluch, Hattush,
3Shecaniah, Rehum, Meremoth,
4Iddo, Ginnethoi, Abijah,
5Mijamin, Maadiah, Bilgah,
6Shemaiah and Joiarib, Jedaiah,
7Sallu, Amok, Hilkiah and Jedaiah.

These were the heads of the priests and their kinsmen in the days of Jeshua.

8The Levites were Jeshua, Binnui, Kadmiel, Sherebiah, Judah, and Mattaniah who was in charge of the songs of thanksgiving, he and his brothers. 9Also Bakbukiah and Unni, their brothers, stood opposite them in their service divisions.

10And Jeshua became the father of Joiakim, and Joiakim became the father of Eliashib, and Eliashib became the father of Joiada, [11]and Joiada became the father of Jonathan, and Jonathan became the father of Jaddua.

[12]Now in the days of Joiakim, the priests, the heads of fathers' households were:

of Seraiah, Meraiah;
of Jeremiah, Hananiah;
[13]of Ezra, Meshullam;
of Amariah, Jehohanan;
[14]of Malluchi, Jonathan;
of Shebaniah, Joseph;
[15]of Harim, Adna;
of Meraioth, Helkai;
[16]of Iddo, Zechariah;
of Ginnethon, Meshullam;
[17]of Abijah, Zichri;
of Miniamin, of Moadiah, Piltai;
[18]of Bilgah, Shammua;
of Shemaiah, Jehonathan;
[19]of Joiarib, Mattenai;
of Jedaiah, Uzzi;
[20]of Sallai, Kallai;
of Amok, Eber;
[21]of Hilkiah, Hashabiah;
of Jedaiah, Nethanel.

[22]As for the Levites, the heads of fathers' households were registered in the days of Eliashib, Joiada, and Johanan and Jaddua; so were the priests in the reign of Darius the Persian. [23]The sons of Levi, the heads of fathers' households, were registered in the Book of the Chronicles up to the days of Johanan the son of Eliashib. [24]The heads of the Levites were Hashabiah, Sherebiah and Jeshua the son of Kadmiel, with their brothers opposite them, to praise and give thanks, as prescribed by David the man of God, division corresponding to division.

[25]Mattaniah, Bakbukiah, Obadiah, Meshullam, Talmon and Akkub were gatekeepers keeping watch at the storehouses of the gates. [26]These served in the days of Joiakim the son of Jeshua, the son of Jozadak, and in the days of Nehemiah the governor and of Ezra the priest and scribe.

[27]Now at the dedication of the wall of Jerusalem they sought out the Levites from all their places, to bring them to Jerusalem so that they might celebrate the dedication with gladness, with hymns of

thanksgiving and with songs to the accompaniment of cymbals, harps and lyres. [28]So the sons of the singers were assembled from the district around Jerusalem, and from the villages of the Netophathites, [29]from Beth-gilgal and from their fields in Geba and Azmaveth, for the singers had built themselves villages around Jerusalem. [30]The priests and the Levites purified themselves; they also purified the people, the gates and the wall.

[31]Then I had the leaders of Judah come up on top of the wall, and I appointed two great choirs, the first proceeding to the right on top of the wall toward the Refuse Gate. [32]Hoshaiah and half of the leaders of Judah followed them, [33]with Azariah, Ezra, Meshullam, [34]Judah, Benjamin, Shemaiah, Jeremiah, [35]and some of the sons of the priests with trumpets; and Zechariah the son of Jonathan, the son of Shemaiah, the son of Mattaniah, the son of Micaiah, the son of Zaccur, the son of Asaph, [36]and his kinsmen, Shemaiah, Azarel, Milalai, Gilalai, Maai, Nethanel, Judah and Hanani, with the musical instruments of David the man of God. And Ezra the scribe went before them. [37]At the Fountain Gate they went directly up the steps of the city of David by the stairway of the wall above the house of David to the Water Gate on the east.

[38]The second choir proceeded to the left, while I followed them with half of the people on the wall, above the Tower of Furnaces, to the Broad Wall, [39]and above the Gate of Ephraim, by the Old Gate, by the Fish Gate, the Tower of Hananel and the Tower of the Hundred, as far as the Sheep Gate; and they stopped at the Gate of the Guard.

[40]Then the two choirs took their stand in the house of God. So did I and half of the officials with me; [41]and the priests, Eliakim, Maaseiah, Miniamin, Micaiah, Elioenai, Zechariah and Hananiah, with the trumpets; [42]and Maaseiah, Shemaiah, Eleazar, Uzzi, Jehohanan, Mal-

chijah, Elam and Ezer. And the singers sang, with Jezrahiah their leader, [43]and on that day they offered great sacrifices and rejoiced because God had given them great joy, even the women and children rejoiced, so that the joy of Jerusalem was heard from afar.

[44]On that day men were also appointed over the chambers for the stores, the contributions, the first fruits and the tithes, to gather into them from the fields of the cities the portions required by the law for the priests and Levites; for Judah rejoiced over the priests and Levites who served. [45]For they performed the worship of their God and the service of purification, together with the singers and the gatekeepers in accordance with the command of David and of his son Solomon. [46]For in the days of David and Asaph, in ancient times, there were leaders of the singers, songs of praise and hymns of thanksgiving to God. [47]So all Israel in the days of Zerubbabel and Nehemiah gave the portions due the singers and the gatekeepers as each day required, and set apart the consecrated portion for the Levites, and the Levites set apart the consecrated portion for the sons of Aaron.

13 [1]On that day they read aloud from the book of Moses in the hearing of the people; and there was found written in it that no Ammonite or Moabite should ever enter the assembly of God, [2]because they did not meet the sons of Israel with bread and water, but hired Balaam against them to curse them. However, our God turned the curse into a blessing. [3]So when they heard the law, they excluded all foreigners from Israel.

[4]Now prior to this, Eliashib the priest, who was appointed over the chambers of the house of our God, being related to Tobiah, [5]had prepared a large room for him, where formerly they put the grain offerings, the frankincense, the utensils and the tithes of grain, wine and oil prescribed for the Levites, the singers and the gatekeepers,

and the contributions for the priests.

⁶But during all this time I was not in Jerusalem, for in the thirty-second year of Artaxerxes king of Babylon I had gone to the king. After some time, however, I asked leave from the king, ⁷and I came to Jerusalem and learned about the evil that Eliashib had done for Tobiah, by preparing a room for him in the courts of the house of God. ⁸It was very displeasing to me, so I threw all of Tobiah's household goods out of the room. ⁹Then I gave an order and they cleansed the rooms; and I returned there the utensils of the house of God with the grain offerings and the frankincense.

¹⁰I also discovered that the portions of the Levites had not been given them, so that the Levites and the singers who performed the service had gone away, each to his own field. ¹¹So I reprimanded the officials and said, "Why is the house of God forsaken?" Then I gathered them together and restored them to their posts.

¹²All Judah then brought the tithe of the grain, wine and oil into the storehouses. ¹³In charge of the storehouses I appointed Shelemiah the priest, Zadok the scribe, and Pedaiah of the Levites, and in addition to them was Hanan the son of Zaccur, the son of Mattaniah; for they were considered reliable, and it was their task to distribute to their kinsmen.

¹⁴Remember me for this, O my God, and do not blot out my loyal deeds which I have performed for the house of my God and its services.

¹⁵In those days I saw in Judah some who were treading wine presses on the sabbath, and bringing in sacks of grain and loading them on donkeys, as well as wine, grapes, figs and all kinds of loads, and they brought them into Jerusalem on the sabbath day. So I admonished them on the day they sold food. ¹⁶Also men of Tyre were living there who imported fish and all kinds of merchandise, and sold them to the sons of Judah on the sabbath, even in Jerusalem. ¹⁷Then I reprimanded the

nobles of Judah and said to them, "What is this evil thing you are doing, by profaning the sabbath day? [18]"Did not your fathers do the same, so that our God brought on us and on this city all this trouble? Yet you are adding to the wrath on Israel by profaning the sabbath."

[19]It came about that just as it grew dark at the gates of Jerusalem before the sabbath, I commanded that the doors should be shut and that they should not open them until after the sabbath. Then I stationed some of my servants at the gates so that no load would enter on the sabbath day. [20]Once or twice the traders and merchants of every kind of merchandise spent the night outside Jerusalem. [21]Then I warned them and said to them, "Why do you spend the night in front of the wall? If you do so again, I will use force against you." From that time on they did not come on the sabbath. [22]And I commanded the Levites that they should purify themselves and come as gatekeepers to sanctify the sabbath day.

For this also remember me, O my God, and have compassion on me according to the greatness of Your lovingkindness.

[23]In those days I also saw that the Jews had married women from Ashdod, Ammon and Moab. [24]As for their children, half spoke in the language of Ashdod, and none of them was able to speak the language of Judah, but the language of his own people. [25]So I contended with them and cursed them and struck some of them and pulled out their hair, and made them swear by God, "You shall not give your daughters to their sons, nor take of their daughters for your sons or for yourselves. [26]"Did not Solomon king of Israel sin regarding these things? Yet among the many nations there was no king like him, and he was loved by his God, and God made him king over all Israel; nevertheless the foreign women caused even him to sin. [27]"Do we then hear about you that you have committed all this great evil by acting unfaithfully against our

God by marrying foreign women?"

[28]Even one of the sons of Joiada, the son of Eliashib the high priest, was a son-in-law of Sanballat the Horonite, so I drove him away from me.

[29]Remember them, O my God, because they have defiled the priesthood and the covenant of the priesthood and the Levites. [30]Thus I purified them from everything foreign and appointed duties for the priests and the Levites, each in his task, [31]and I arranged for the supply of wood at appointed times and for the first fruits.

Remember me, O my God, for good.

NOTES

Chapter Five
1. Helen Howarth Lemmel, "Turn Your Eyes Upon Jesus," 1922.

Chapter Seven
1. Don Shirley, "Gwen Verdon; Dancer, Actress Won 4 Tony Awards in 6 Years," *LA Times*, October 19, 2000.

Chapter Thirteen
1. Katherine B. Weissman, "Home of the Brave," *O The Oprah Magazine*, February 2001, 133.